New Series February/March 1993
Volume 32 / Numbers 11 & 12
Edited by Alan Ross
Deputy Editor: Jeremy Lewis

London

GW00726037

Subscriptions £28.50 ($67) p.a. to *London Magazine,* 30 Thurloe Place, SW7. Subscription renewals, etc: Bailey Brothers, 127 Sandgate Road, Folkestone, Kent. Contributions must be accompanied by a stamped addressed envelope or International Reply Coupons. Advertising: 589 0618. We acknowledge the financial assistance of the Arts Council.

© *London Magazine* 1992.

Printed by Shenval Print Ltd of Harlow

The Dream Lover

'None of these girls is French, right?'

'No. But they're European.'

'Not the same thing, man. French is crucial.'

'Of course . . .' I don't know what he is talking about but it seems politic to agree.

'You know any French girls?'

'Of course,' I say again. This is almost a lie, but it doesn't matter at this stage.

'But *well*? I mean well enough to ask out?'

'I don't see why not.' Now this time we are well into mendacity, but I am unconcerned. I feel good, adult, quite confident today. This lie can germinate and grow for a while.

I am standing in a pale parallelogram of March sunshine, leaning against a wall, talking to my American friend, Preston. The wall belongs to the Centre Universitaire Méditerranéan, a large stuccoed Villa on the promenade at Nice. In front of us is a small cobbled courtyard bounded by a balustrade. Beyond is the Promenade des Anglais, its four lanes busy with Nice's traffic. Over the burnished roofs of the cars I can see the Mediterranean. The Baie des Anges looks grey and grimy in this season: old, tired water – ashy, cindery.

'We got to do something . . .' Preston says, a hint of petulant desperation in his voice. I like the 'we'. Preston scratches his short hard hair noisily. 'What with the new apartment, and all.'

'You moved out of the hotel?'

'Yeah. Want to come by tonight?' He shifts his big frame as if troubled by a fugitive itch, and pats his pockets – breast, hip, thigh – looking for his cigarettes. 'We got a bar on the roof.'

I am intrigued, but I explain that the invitation has to be turned down as it is a Monday, and every Monday night I have a dinner appointment with a French family – friends of friends of my mother.

Preston shrugs, then finds and sets fire to a cigarette. He smokes an American brand called 'Picayune' which is made in New Orleans.

When he came to France he brought two thousand with him. He has never smoked anything else since he was fourteen, he insists.

We watch our fellow students saunter into the building. They are nearly all strangers to me, these bright boys and girls, as I have only been in Nice a few weeks, and, so far, Preston is the only friend I have made. Slightly envious of their easy conviviality, I watch the others chatter and mingle – Germans, Scandinavians, Italians, Tunisians, Nigerians . . . We are all foreigners, trying hard to learn French and win our diplomas . . . Except for Preston, who makes no effort at all and seems quite content to remain monoglot.

A young guy with long hair rides his motorbike into the courtyard. He is wearing no shirt. He is English and, apart from me, the only other English person in the place. He revs his motobike unnecessarily a few times before parking it and switching it off. He takes a T-shirt out of a saddle bag and nonchalantly pulls it on. I think how I too would like to own a motorbike and do exactly what he has done . . . His name is Tim. One day, I imagine, we might be friends. We'll see.

*   *   *

Monsieur Cambrai welcomes me with his usual exhausting, impossible geniality. He shakes my hand fervently and shouts to his wife over his shoulder.

'Ne bouge pas. C'est l'habitué. L'habitué!'

That's what he calls me – l'habitué, l'habitué de lundi, to give the appellation in full, so called because I am invited to dinner every Monday night without fail. He almost never uses my proper name and sometimes I find this perpetual alias a little wearing, a little stressful. 'Salut, l'habitué', 'Bien mangé, l'habitué? 'Encore du vin, l'habitué?', and so on. But I like him and the entire Cambrai family; in fact I like them so much that it makes me feel weak, insufficient, cowed.

Monsieur and Madame are small people, fit, sophisticated and nimble, with neat spry figures. Both of them are dentists, it so happens, who teach at the big medical school here in Nice. A signifi- cant portion of my affection for them owes to the fact that they have three daughters – Delphine, Stephane and Annique – all older than me and all possessed of – to my fogged and blurry eyes – an incandescent, almost supernatural beauty. Stephane and Annique still live with their parents. Delphine has a flat somewhere in the city, but she often dines at home. These are the French girls that I claimed to know, though 'know' is far too inadequate a word to sum up the complexity of my feelings for them. I come to their house on Monday nights as a supplicant and votary, both frightened and in awe of them. I sit in their luminous presence, quiet and eager, for two hours or so, unmanned by my astonishing good fortune.

I am numbed further when I consider the family's disarming, disinterested kindness. When I arrived in Nice they were the only contacts I had in the city and, on my mother's urging, I duly wrote to them citing our tenuous connection via my mother's friend. To my surprise I was promptly invited to dinner and then invited back every Monday night. What shamed me was that I knew I myself could never be so hospitable so quickly, not even to a close friend, and what was more I knew no one else who would be, either. So I cross the Cambrai threshold each Monday with a rich cocktail of emotions gurgling inside me: shame, guilt, gratitude, admiration and – it goes without saying – lust.

*   *   *

Preston's new address is on the Promenade des Anglais itself – the 'Résidence Les Anges'. I stand outside the building, looking up, impressed. I have passed it many times before, a distressing and vulgar edifice on this celebrated boulevard, an unadorned rectangle of coppery, smoked glass with stacked ranks of gilded aluminium balconies.

I press a buzzer in a slim, freestanding concrete post and speak into a crackling wire grille. When I mention the name 'Mr Fairfield' glass doors part softly and I am admitted to a bare granite lobby where a taciturn man in a tight suit shows me to the lift.

Preston rents a small studio apartment with a bathroom and kitchenette. It is a neat, pastel coloured and efficient module. On the wall are a series of prints of exotic birds: a toucan, a bataleur eagle, something called a blue shrike. As I stand there looking round I think of my own temporary home, my thin room in Madame d'Amico's ancient, dim apartment, and the inefficient and bathless bathroom I have to share with her other lodgers, and a sudden hot envy rinses through me. I half hear Preston enumerating the various financial consequences of his tenancy: how much this studio costs a month; the outrageous supplement he had to pay even to rent it in the first place; and how he had been obliged to cash in his return fare to the States (first class) in order to˙meet it. He says he has called his father for more money.

We ride up to the roof, six storeys above the Promenade. To my vague alarm there is a small swimming pool up here and a large glassed in cabaña – furnished with a bamboo bar and some rattan seats – labled 'Club Les Anges' in neon copperplate. A barman in a short cerise jacket runs this place, a portly, pale faced fellow with a poor moustache whose name is Serge. Although Preston jokes patronisingly with him it is immediately quite clear to me both that Serge loathes Preston and that Preston is completely unaware of this powerful animus directed against him.

I order a large gin and tonic from Serge and for a shrill palpilating minute I loathe Preston too. I know there are many better examples on offer, of course, but for the time being this shiny building and its accoutrements will do nicely as an approximation of The Good Life for me. And as I sip my sour drink a sour sense of the world's huge unfairness crowds ruthlessly on. Why should this guileless, big American, barely older than me, with his two thousand Lousiana cigarettes, and his cashable first-class air tickets have all *this* . . . while I live in a narrow frowsty room in an old woman's decrepit apartment? (My straightened circumstances are caused by a seemingly interminable postal strike in Britain that means money cannot be transferred to my Nice account and I have to husband my financial resources like a neurotic peasant conscious of a hard winter lowering ahead.) Where is *my* money, I want to know, *my* exotic bird prints, *my* pool? How long will I have to wait before these artefacts become the commonplace of my life? . . . I allow this unpleasant voice to whine and whinge on in my head as we stand on the terrace and admire the view of the long bay. One habit I have already learnt, even at my age, is not to resist these fervent grudges – give them a loose rein, let them run themselves out, it is always better in the longer run.

In fact I am drawn to Preston, and want him to be my friend. He is tall and powerfully built – the word 'rangey' comes to mind – affable and not particularly intelligent. To my eyes his clothes are so parodically American as to be beyond caricature: pale blue baggy shirts with button-down collars, old khaki trousers short enough to reveal his white-socked ankles and big brown loafers. He has a gold watch, a zippo lighter and an ugly ring with a red stone set in it. He told me once, in all candour, in all modesty, that he 'played tennis to Davis Cup standard'.

I always wondered what he was doing in Nice, studying at the Centre. At first I thought he might be a draftee avoiding the war in Vietnam but I now suspect – based on some hints he has dropped – that he has been sent off to France as an obscure punishment of some sort. His family don't want him at home: he has done something wrong and these months in Nice are his penance.

But hardly an onerous one, that's for sure: he has no interest in his classes – those he can be bothered to take – nor in the language and culture of France. He simply has to endure this exile and he will be allowed home where, I imagine, he will resume his soft life of casual privilege and unreflecting ease once more. He talks a good deal about his eventual return to the States where he plans to impose his own particular punishment, or extract his own special reward. He says he will force his father to buy him an Aston Martin. His father will have no say in the matter, he remarks with untypical vehemence and determination. He will have his Aston Martin, and it is the bright promise of this glossy English car that really seems to sustain him through these dog days on the Mediterranean littoral.

*　　　　*　　　　*

Soon I find I am a regular visitor at ther Résidence Les Anges, where I go most afternoons after my classes are over. Preston and I sit in the club, or by the pool if it is sunny, and drink. We consume substantial amounts (it all goes on his tab) and consequently I am usually fairly drunk by sunset. Our conversation ranges far and wide but at some point in every discussion Preston reiterates his desire to meet French girls. If I do indeed know some French girls, he says, why don't I ask them to the club? I reply that I am working on it, and coolly change the subject.

Steadily, over the days, I learn more about my American friend. He is an only child. His father (who has not responded to his requests for money) is a millionaire – real estate. His mother divorced him recently to marry another, richer millionaire. Between his two sets of millionaire parents Preston has a choice of eight homes to visit in and around the USA: in Miami, New York, Palm Springs and a ranch in Montana. Preston dropped out of college after two semesters and does not work.

'Why should I?' he argues reasonably. 'They've got more than enough money for me too. Why should I bust my ass working trying to earn more?'

'But isn't it . . What do you do all day?'

'All kinds of shit . . . But mostly I like to play tennis a lot. And I like to fuck, of course.'

'So why did you come to Nice?'

He grins. 'I was a bad boy.' He slaps his wrist and laughs. 'Naughty, naughty Preston.'

He won't tell me what he did.

* * *

It is Spring in Nice. Each day we start to enjoy a little more sunshine and whenever it appears within ten minutes there is a particular girl, lying on the plage publique in front of the centre, sunbathing. Often I stand and watch her spread out there, still, supine on the cool pebbles – the only sunbather along the entire bay. It turns out she is well known, that this is a phenomenon that occurs every year. By early summer her tan is solidly established and she is very brown indeed. By August she is virtually black, with that kind of dense, matt tan, the life burned out of the skin, her pores brimming with melanin. Her ambition each year, they say, is to be the brownest girl on the Cote d'Azur . . .

I watch her lying there, immobile beneath the invisible rain of ultra violet. It is definitely not warm – even in my jacket and scarf I shiver slightly in the fresh breeze. How can she be bothered? I wonder, but at the same time I have to admit there is something admirable in such singlemindedness, such ludicrous dedication.

*   *   *

Eventually I take my first girl to the Club to meet Preston. Her name is Ingrid, she is in my class, a Norwegian, but with dark auburn hair. I don't know her well but she seems a friendly, uncomplicated soul. She speaks perfect English and German.

'Are you French?' Preston asks, almost immediately.

Ingrid is very amused by this. 'I'm Norwegian,' she explains. 'Is it important?'

I apologise to Preston when Ingrid goes off to change into her swimming costume, but he waves it away, not to worry he says, she's cute. Ingrid returns and we sit in the sun and order the first of our many drinks. Ingrid, after some prompting, smokes one of Preston's Picayune cigarettes. The small flaw that emerges to mar our pleasant afternoon is that, the more Ingrid drinks, so does her conversation become dominated by references to a French boy she is seeing called Jean-Jacques. Preston hides his disappointment; he is the acme of good manners.

Later, we play poker using cheese biscuits as chips. Ingrid sits opposite me in her her multicoloured swimsuit. She is plumper than I had imagined, and I decide that if I had to sum her up in one word it would be 'homely'. Except for one detail: she has very hairy arm-pits. On one occasion she sits back in her chair, studying her cards for a full minute, her free hand idly scratching a bite on the back of her neck. Both Preston's and my eyes are drawn to the thick divot of auburn hair that is revealed by this gesture: we stare at it, fascinated, as Ingrid deliberates whether to call or raise.

After she has gone Preston confesses that he found her unshavenness quite erotic. I am not so sure.

That night we sit on in the Club long into the night, as usual the place's sole customers, with Serge unsmilingly replenishing our drinks as Preston calls for them. Ingrid's presence, the unwitting erotic charge that she has detonated in our normally tranquil, bibulous afternoons, seems to have unsettled and troubled Preston somewhat and without any serious prompting on my part he tells me why he has come to Nice. He informs me that the man his mother remarried was a widower, an older man, with four children already in their twenties. When Preston dropped out of college he went to stay with his mother and new stepfather. He exhales, he eats several olives, his face goes serious and solemn for a moment.

'This man, his name's Michael, had three daughters – and a son, who was already married – and, man, you should have seen those girls.' He grins, a stupid, gormless grin. 'I was eighteen years old and I got three beautiful girls sleeping down the corridor from me. What am I supposed to do?'

The answer, unvoiced, seemed to slip into the Club like a draught of air. I felt my spine tauten.

'You mean – ?'

'Yeah, sure. All three of them. Eventually.'

I don't want to speak, so I think through this. I imagine a big silent house, night, long dark corridors, closed doors. Three bored blonde tanned stepsisters. Suddenly there's a tall young man in the house, a virtual stranger, who plays tennis to David Cup standard.

'What went wrong?' I manage.

'Oldest one, Janie, got pregnant, didn't she? Last year.'

'Abortion?'

'Are you kidding? She just married her fiancé real fast.'

'You mean she was engaged when –'

'He doesn't know a thing. But she told my mother.'

'The, the child was –'

'Haven't seen him yet.' He turns and calls for Serge. 'No one knows, no one suspects . . .' He grins again. 'Until the kid starts smoking Picayunes.' He reflects on his life a moment, and turns his big mild face to me. 'That's why I'm here. Keeping my head down. Not exactly flavour of the month back home.'

*   *   *

The next girl I take to the Club is also a Scandinavian – we have eight
in our class – but this time a Swede, called Danni. Danni is very
attractive and vivacious, in my opinion, with straight white-blonde
hair. She's a tall girl, full breasted, and she would be perfect but for
the fact that she has one slightly withered leg, noticeably thinner than
the other, which causes her to limp. She is admirably unselfconscious
about her disability.

'Hi,' Preston says, 'are you French?'

Danni hides her increculity. 'Mais, oui, monsieur. Bien sur.' Like
Ingrid, she finds this presumption highly amusing. Preston soon
realizes his mistake, and makes light of his disappointment.

Danni wears a small cobalt bikini and even swims in the pool, which
is freezing. (Serge says there is something wrong with the heating
mechanism but we don't believe him.) Danni's fortitude impresses
Preston: I can see it in his eyes, as he watches her dry herself. He asks
her what happened to her leg and she tells him she had polio as a
child.

'Shit, you were lucky you don't need a caliper.'

This breaks the ice and we soon get noisily drunk, much to
Serge's irritation. But there is little he can do as there is no one else in
the Club who might complain. Danni produces some grass and we
blatantly smoke a joint. Typically, apart from faint nausea, the drug
has not the slightest effect on me, but it afford Serge a chance to be
officious and as he clears away a round of empty glasses he says to
Preston, 'Ça va pas, monsieur, non, non, ça va pas.'

'Fuck you, Serge,' he says amiably and Danni's unstoppable blurt of
laughter sets us all off. I sense Serge's humiliation and realize the
relationship with Preston is changing fast: the truculent deference has
gone; the dislike is overt, almost a challenge.

After Danni has left, Preston tells me about his latest money problems. His bar bill at the Club now stands at over $400 and the man-
agement is insisting it be settled. His father won't return his calls,
acknowledge telegrams and Preston has no credit cards. He is contem-
plating pawning his watch in order to pay something into the
account and defer suspicion. I buy it off him for 500 francs.

*   *   *

I look around my class counting the girls I know. I know most of them by now, well enough to talk to. Both Ingrid and Danni have been back to the club and have enthused about their afternoons there, and I realize that to my fellow students I have become an object of some curiosity as a result of my unexpected ability to dispense these small doses of luxury and decadence: the exclusive addresses, the privacy of the club, the pool on the roof, the endless flow of free drinks . . .

Preston decided to abandon his French classes a while ago and I am now his sole link with the Centre. It is with some mixed emotions – I feel vaguely pimp-like, oddly smirched – that I realize how simple it is to attract girls to the Club Les Anges.

*   *   *

Annique Cambrai is the youngest of the Cambrai daughters and the closest to me in age. She is only two years older than me but seems considerably more than that. I was, I confess, oddly daunted by her mature good looks, dark with a lean, attractive face, and because of this at first I think she found me rather aloof, but now, after many Monday dinners, we have become more relaxed and friendly. She is studying law at the University of Nice and speaks good English with a marked American accent. When I comment on this she explains that most French universities now offer you a choice of accents when you study English and, like ninety per cent of students, she has chosen American.

I see my opportunity and take it immediately: would she, I diffidently enquire, like to come to the Résidence Les Anges to meet an American friend of mine and perhaps try her new accent out on him?

The next morning, on my way down the rue de France to the Centre I see Preston standing outside a pharmacy reading the *Herald Tribune*. I call his name and cross the road to tell him the excellent news about Annique.

'You won't believe this,' I say, 'But I finally got a real French girl.'

Preston's face looks odd: half a smile, half a morose grimace of disappointment.

'That's great,' he says, dully, 'wonderful.'

A tall, slim girl steps out of the pharmacy and hands him a plastic bag.

'This is Lois,' he says. We shake hands.

I know who Lois is, Preston has often spoken of her: my damn-near fiancée, he calls her. It transpires that Lois has flown over spontaneously and unannounced to visit him.

'And, boy, are my Mom and Dad mad as hell,' she laughs.

Lois is a pretty girl, with a round, innocent face quite free of make up. She is tall, even in her sneakers she is as tall as me, with a head of incredibly thick, dense brown hair which, for some reason, I associate particularly with American girls. I feel sure also, though as yet I have no evidence, that she is a very clean person – physically clean, I mean to say – someone who showers and washes regularly, redolent of soap and the lingering farinaceous odour of talcum powder.

I stroll back with them to the Résidence. Lois's arrival has temporarily solved Preston's money problems: they have cashed in her return ticket and paid off the bar bill and the next quarter's rent which had come due. Preston feels rich enough to buy back his watch from me.

*　　*　　*

Annique looks less mature and daunting in her swimsuit, I'm pleased to say, though I was disappointed that she favoured a demure apple-green one-piece. The pool's heater has been 'fixed' and for the first time we all swim in the small azure rectangle – Preston and Lois, Annique and me. It is both strange and exciting for me to see Annique so comparatively unclothed and even stranger to lie side by side, thigh by thigh, inches apart, sunbathing.

Lois obviously assumes Annique and I are a couple – a quite natural assumption under the circumstances, I suppose – she would never imagine I had brought her for Preston. I keep catching him gazing at Annique, and a mood of frustration and intense sadness seems to emanate from him – a mood of which only I am aware. And in turn a peculiar exhilaration builds inside me, not just because of Lois's innocent assumption about my relation to Annique, but also because I know now that I have succeeded. I have brought Preston the perfect French girl: Annique, by his standards, represents the paradigm, the Platonic ideal for this American male. Here she is, unclothed, lying by his pool, in his club, drinking his drinks, but he can do nothing – and what makes my own excitement grow is the realization that for the first time in our friendship – perhaps for the first time in his life – Preston envies another person. Me.

*   *   *

Now that Lois has arrived I stay away from the Résidence Les Anges. It won't be the same again and, despite my secret delight, I don't want to taunt Preston with the spectre of Annique. But I find that without the spur of his envy the tender fantasy inevitably dims; for my dream life, my dream love, to flourish, I need to share it with Preston. I decide to pay a visit. Preston opens the door of his studio.

'Hi stranger,' he says, with some enthusiasm. 'Am I glad to see you.' He seems sincere. I follow him into the apartment. The small room is untidy, the bed unmade, the floor strewn with female clothes. I hear the noise of the shower from the bathroom: Lois may be a clean person but it is clear she is also something of a slut.

'How are things with Annique?' he asks, almost at once, as casually as he can manage. He has to ask, I know it.

I look at him .'Good.' I let the pause develop, pregnant with innuendo. 'No, they're good.'

His nostrils flare and he shakes his head.

'God, you're one lucky –'

Lois comes in from the bathroom in a dressing gown, towelling her thick hair dry.

'Hi, Edward,' she says, 'what's new?' Then she sits down on the bed and begins to weep.

We stand and look at her as she sobs quietly.

'It's nothing,' Preston says. 'She just wants to go home.' He tells me that neither of them has left the building for eight days. They are completely, literally, penniless. Lois's parents have cancelled her credit cards and collect calls home have failed to produce any response. Preston has been unable to locate his father and now his stepfather refuses to speak to him (a worrying sign) and although his mother would like to help she is powerless for the moment, given Preston's fall from grace. Preston and Lois have been living on a diet of olives, peanuts and cheese biscuits served up in the bar and, of course, copious alcohol.

'Yeah, but now we're even banned from there,' Lois says, with an unfamiliar edge to her voice.

'Last night I beat up on that fuckwit, Serge,' Preston explains with a shrug. 'Something I had to do.'

He goes on to enumerate their other problems: their bar bill stands at over $300; Serge is threatening to go to the police unless he is compensated; the management has grown hostile and suspicious.

'We got to get out of here,' Lois says miserably. 'I hate it here, I hate it.'

Preston turns to me. 'Can you help us out?' he says. I feel the laugh erupt within me.

*   *   *

I stand in Nice station and hand Preston two train tickets to Luxembourg and two one-way Iceland Air tickets to New York. Lois reaches out to touch them as if they were sacred relics.

'You've got a six-hour wait in Reykjavic for your connection,' I tell him, 'but, believe me, there is no cheaper way to fly.'

I bask in their voluble gratitude for a while. They have no luggage with them as they could not be seen to be quitting the Résidence. Preston says his father is now in New York and assures me I will be reimbursed the day they arrive. I have spent almost everything I possess on these tickets, but I don't care – I am intoxicated with my own generosity and the strange power it has conferred on me. Lois leaves us to go in search of a toilette and Preston embraces me in a clumsy hug. 'I won't forget this, man,' he says many times. We celebrate our short but intense friendship and affirm its continuance, but all the while I am waiting for him to ask me – I can feel the question growing in his head like a tumour. Through the crowds of passengers we see Lois making her way back. He doesn't have much time left.

'Listen,' he begins, his voice low, 'did you and Annique . . .? I mean, are you–'

'We've been looking for an apartment. That's why you haven't seen much of me.'

'Jesus . . .'

Lois calls out something about the train timetable, but we are not listening. Preston seems to be trembling, he turns away, and when he turns back I see the pale fires of impotent resentment light his eyes.

'Are you fucking her?'

'Why else would we be looking for an apartment?'

'What's going on?' Lois asks. 'The train's leaving soon.'

Preston gestures at me, as if he can't pronounce my name. 'Annique . . . They're moving in together.'

Lois squeals. She's so pleased, she really is, she really really likes Annique.

By the time I see them onto the train Preston has calmed down and our final farewells are sincere. He looks around the modest station intently as if trying to record its essence, as if now he wished to preserve something of this city he inhabited so complacently, with such absence of curiosity.

'God, it's too bad,' he says with an exquisite fervour. 'I know I could have liked Nice. I *know*. I really could.'

I back off, wordless, this is too good, this is too generous of him. This is perfect.

'Give my love to Annique,' Preston says quietly, as Lois calls loud goodbyes.

'Oh, don't worry,' I say, looking at Preston. 'I will.'

Further stories by:

William Bedford ∗ Stephen Blanchard
E. A. Markham ∗ Sheridan Keith
Richard Madelin ∗ Rachel Blake

Melters

It was some little time after he had started at the Steel Works before Arthur had occasion to visit the Siemens Furnaces where his father worked. He had to climb an outside iron stairway to reach the Siemens platform, half way up a giant shed. The platform ran the length of the shed but was built to cover one half of the shed width only. On the other side, at ground level, were the casting pits.

On the edge of the platform, overlooking the pits, were the five Siemens furnaces with their spouts or 'launders' projecting a little way over the edge.

When the steel was ready for teeming, it was run down one of the spouts into a giant ladle.

The furnacemen − smelters or 'melters' as they were known − worked on the platform. The furnace hearths were on the opposite side to the spouts, facing onto the main breadth of the platform. While the steel was being made, a period of eight hours or more for each furnace charge, the 'melters' worked almost entirely on the hearth side of the furnace.

The furnaces were made of a steel shell, lined with refractory bricks and rammed burnt dolomite. Each furnace on the landing worked as an independent unit. As a rule four furnaces were engaged in steel making while the fifth was being relined.

Arthur could see his father down the length of the great shed, near the glare of Number Three furnace. The lofty walls and the shed roof were barely visible in the gloom; such skylights as were present in more normal times had been blacked out because of the war. Arthur moved carefully forward along the platform.

Jabez Brown looked through the open mouth of Number Three furnace into the seething, molten mass beyond. He held a strip of dark blue glass before his eyes; had he not used it the glare from the furnace would have blinded him. By the appearance of the molten metal and of the gases swirling above, he could make a good estimate of the stage reached in the steel-making.

These days everything was calculated to a fraction, all worked out by the brains trust in the laboratory. But Jabez could tell near enough. He could tell when to take a sample or when the steel was ready for teeming. He didn't need his pocket watch; he could sense it. Not that he begrudged the laboratory lads their fun. Jabez knew well that what with slide-rules and modern chemistry and figures, with different degrees of carburizing and ferro-silicon alloys, there was more to it than he would ever know. As he sometimes confided to his fellow melters: 'It's th' book·werk that's got we skint –' He replaced the strip of blue glass in a waistcoat pocket. The First Hand Smelter was ''avin a day's play'. His son was home from Malta for the first time in four years. Jabez being Second Hand naturally took over the responsibility of the furnace. The Third Hand Smelter moved up one, a 'by-turn' man stepped up to Third Hand and another labourer was found by the Plant Manager to complete the team at work on the furnace. Jabez walked deliberately to the back of the Siemens' shed and pulled a lever forwards. It was one of a series somewhat similar to the levers in a railway signal box. The furnace door, worked by hydraulic pressure, sank slowly into place. The door was faced with special heat-resisting bricks and as it closed, the roar of the furnace was damped down and the heat and glare greatly reduced.

To Arthur, watching the spectacle for the first time, it seemed that the world was suddenly plunged into darkness. It was almost a minute before he became used to the change and began to pick out objects in the pale electric light. Arthur started at the sudden scream of nearby machinery. A crane driver, high in the gloom overhead, sent his seventy-five tons of metal rolling along its track down the length of the great shed. Arthur pressed himself against the grimy iron sheeting of the shed wall as the monster slid by, a yard or so distant. He felt a sudden grip on his arm and found Jabez beside him, an islet of security amid this maze of modern danger. His father's face seemed pale and unreal. The light bulbs stretched away on either side overhead, like street lamps in a fog. In front of him, twenty yards distant, Number Three Furnace pulsated like a live thing, throwing out little shafts and lines of red light between the containing steel plates.

Fancy having to walk right up to the furnace with the door lifted, like his father did, thought Arthur. He felt the top of his scalp prickling.

'Us'll goo rahnd t'other side,' said Jabez. 'Watch whee-er I goo,' he admonished Arthur. He started off with sure tread across the heavy boards.

Arthur followed warily, picking his way round small heaps of bricks, sand and dolomite and over a stack of tubular construction sections. As he approached the furnace the heat increased until he felt the sweat start from his pores. He followed Jabez round the end of the furnace. The heat seemed suffocating. He felt the blast on his right cheek. The furnace wall, six feet away, seemed to him too fragile and insecure to contain such a burden. Why, the plates themselves were red hot.

It occurred to Arthur that his father was being very foolhardy in getting so close to this monster. It was filled with a menacing power of destruction. If something were to go wrong and the furnace cracked open – as it seemed capable of doing any moment – the molten contents would spurt out and they would perish in hideous agony. He little knew at the time how right he was to be so wary.

Arthur followed his father carefully with tentative steps. As well as the feeling of danger there was also a spice of excitement. This began to grip him more and more as he became accustomed to the strange conditions.

'Stand by 'ere, ow-er Art,' Jabez told him, indicating an oasis of security amid the desert of incalculable hazard. They were at the back of the furnace now, on a gangway perhaps six feet wide, littered with numerous impedimenta. At the edge of this was a great gaping chasm. It was like coming suddenly to the edge of a precipice.

Along the edge, placed as though haphazard, were short sections of tubular guard fencing. It was near one of these that Arthur now stood.

A gaunt figure appeared out of the murk at the side of the furnace. He was a giant of a man with a grimed, emotionless face like some strange figure from a wax-works show. He wore the cloth cap, knotted kerchief, waistcoat, corduroy trousers and heavy boots of the typical steel worker, covered by layers of dust and ash. He moved up to Jabez with ponderous tread and spoke into his ear.

'Be 'er ready?' he asked.

Jabez had been signalling to some other confederate in this new bemusing world. He spoke over his shoulder.

'Ar,' said Jabez.

As the gaunt man passed Arthur, he favoured him with a brief nod before ascending a short flight of steps to the nearby 'pulpit' where the furnace-tilting mechanism was housed. Arthur looked down from the platform onto the scene below. Daylight was filtering in through a gap where a section of the far wall had been swung back.

Below him was what seemed to be a railway siding. Grouped on the platforms on either side of the track, were huge cylinders, like collections of massive milk churns. They were the moulds for making the two and a half ton steel ingots. Scattered about in heaps and massive stacks were numbers of the formed ingots themselves.

Some way off in the chasm below, a giant ladle was being hooked onto the chain cable of a bridge crane. This reached high overhead and dwarfed even the platform crane in size. Two men were holding up the handle of the great ladle with iron bars. As Arthur watched the men lowered their pikes, allowing the handle of the ladle to drop onto the great hook which had been manoeuvered into position. A hand was raised, there was a grinding of machinery as the slack of the cable was taken up, a pause with the handle now upright, another wave and the ladle was lifted vertically with a harsh grinding from above. It hung there for a few seconds like a great basket and then, with a scream of wheels, the whole bridge of the crane moved towards Number Three Furnace, swinging the massive ladle like a toy. With practiced artistry it was manoeuvered into place, poised over the correct spot and finally lowered, almost without a jar, to a position directly below the spout of the furnace, ready to receive the molten steel.

Arthur heard a hoarse shout as Jabez gave the word to his Second Hand. After a few moments heavy machinery began to growl behind him.

Slowly, almost imperceptibly at first, the furnace tilted over like a great ship swaying gently onto its side. After a short pause a few molten drops spilled into the launder. Following these the steel came in a steady, white-hot trickle. The trickle soon became a small stream; the stream a cascade. The heat and glare once more became intense as the blinding lava-like flow leapt clear of the culvert in a graceful arc and spilled into the waiting ladle below amid showers of red and orange sparks and billows of white smoke.

Arthur, though hot in body, was once more frozen into immobility.

The gaunt giant reappeared. He stood not four feet from the molten stream, leaning casually on a shovel. A splash of metal was thrown onto one of the platform planks. He swept up some sand onto his shovel from a pile at his feet, dropped it onto the smouldering splash in one smooth movement and was back leaning on his shovel in four seconds.

As more and more steel ran from the furnace the heat and glare from the ladle increased and the air was thick with pungent white fumes. The heat was so intense that Arthur had to step back from the platform's edge.

When the ladle was about half full, Jabez casually picked up some slim metal bars apparently lying haphazard near the edge. He strolled nearer until he was barely a yard from the spout and, after watching for a moment or so, cast the aluminium, for such it was, into the seething cauldron. The previous sparks were insignificant compared with the showers of stars which now rose in a magnificent display from the ladle. Jabez turned back as though pleased with the effect and having collected four more bars, repeated the manoeuvre.

Arthur watched the two impassive figures, his father and the gaunt Second Hand. They were typical of the skilled workmen of the steel trade. Slow, almost ponderous, yet alert and sure in action. Confident yet watchful. They knew their job and did not underestimate its constant dangers. He was destined to discover that such knowledge was not easy to acquire; was sometimes a painful and critically dangerous process. The furnace went on tilting, allowing the remainder of the molten steel, in the curved base, to run out through the teeming hole. Finally the stream dwindled to a trickle, which in its turn died.

The ladle was now ready for the next part of it's journey to a waiting upright mould further down the great shed. Once there, a second chain, already attached to the bottom of the ladle, served to tip it so that metal could be run from its lip into the central chamber of a waiting mould complex. As the central 'trumpet' filled, metal ran into the adjacent surrounding chambers through radial channels, filling them from below. This way of making ingots being known as 'up hill teeming'. Having seen the giant ladle safely on its way, Jabez turned to his son.

'Thee'd best be gettin' whum, lad, and get thee tay,' he said. Arthur tore his eyes away from the scene below.

'Or-reet, Dad,' he agreed.

Jabez led the way back round the furnace. The walls were only glowing a dull red now. Arthur felt more secure. He parted from his father on the gangway, near the lights. Jabez was on the afternoon shift.

'Ke'p on this side till yo'm near th' ladder.' They parted with a mutual smile.

Arthur stepped prudently along the planking, found his way down the iron ladder and set off towards the main gate across the maze of railway lines.

He picked his way along winding paths between huts, stacks, sheds and strange gigantic contraptions. Beside the path were billets, planks, tubular sections, odds and ends of steel cuttings, stacks of bricks and unidentifiable heaps, all covered with a liberal layer of black grime.

The grime covered the stacks and buildings, the railway tracks and lines; it lay, inches thick, between the sleepers; it hung in the air and was blown about by the wind; it fell onto Arthur Brown's carefully tended hair and specs of it got into his eyes. He was relieved when he had passed the Blast Furnaces and the air became a little clearer.

As he swung along with his hands in his pockets his mind was still filled with the vivid scenes he had just witnessed. There was a danger and something of thrill in Jabez' work he had never before appreciated. His heart warmed to his father. All these years and his Dad had never told them; had never let them know what it was really like. That it was one of the hottest and most hazardous jobs on earth. Just: ' 'ad a splash uv metal in me boot' or 'Woi day you cum up th' werks; learn a re-ul job?'

After working in the works' garage for a few weeks, much to his delight, Arthur had been transferred onto a mechanical shover or bull-dozer on the scrap dump. He had been well satisfied with the bull-dozer until he had been 'down th' Siemens'. Now wider vistas began to unfold. There were wonderful machines to be handled in the

Siemens; mechanical chargers, for instance, and best of all those cranes of gigantic size. What a marvellous job that would be, he thought, carrying his head as high as his five-foot-eight would allow. Why the chap in that crane-driver's box, up near the roof, was controlling the whole destiny of the steel. He was all-powerful; king-like. What was even better, his pay was double Arthur's. With that sort of pay he could think of getting his own van with Gildroy. There was the war to finish first, of course, but after . . .

He'd come back to the Steel Works after the war, get his job back – or something better, like crane-driving – and earn some re-ul money. After a year or two, he might even consider settling down. A picture of Pearl Prosser came into his mind. Arthur went on his way, building castles in the smoke.

A fortnight after his introduction to the Siemens Furnaces, Arthur received his call-up papers. When the day came for his medical he was nervous. Apart from the general tension his ear was running again for the first time in months. When he was graded Four – rejected – it was a heavy blow. He had been impatient for the day when he too would be in uniform and able to take his chance with the rest. When he could show some outward sign of his willingness to serve; his gladness to contribute his small share in his country's fight for life. When he could swing down Silver Street in his battle-dress with casual unconcern and savour at least the pride of family and of friends.

The earth was a bitter place to Arthur, after he had been rejected. His mother and Jabez did what they could to make him snap out of it.

'Yo'm mow-er use whee-er yo am, lad,' Jabez would say. 'Ask oo yo please.' Or: 'They'm speakin' well on yo at th' garrige.'

But Arthur would not be consoled. He lay awake at night nursing his disappointment; his sense of loss.

Afterwards he was more than ever determined to get on at the Works. Even so his rejection for the Army lay at the back of his mind like a canker. As the weeks passed and the soreness of the blow eased, a shadow lay across him, spoiling his full enjoyment of life and marring his concentration. At work he felt he would be satisfied with nothing less than one of those big cranes. He spent his time working and scheming for it.

Please

'If you want to keep this job,' he'd said, 'you should try and be nice to me. It's in your interest.'

'I'm your employer,' he'd said. 'And if I tell the immigration authorities I no longer need your services, they'll deport you.'

'All I'd have to do would be to withdraw my guarantee from your work permit,' he'd said, 'and you'll be branded as an illegal alien.'

'It's in your interest not to cross me. It's in your best interests. And anyway,' he'd tried to smile at that point, 'I'd like to think there'd be more in it for you too. Apart from just being in your interest, that is, in a negative way, I mean. I'd like to think you'd find something positive in it as well. Not just something you had to do, but something you'd like to do. Perhaps something more, even than that.'

A corpulent, middle-aged man who wore braces to keep his trousers up. He stuck a pencil behind his ear as he poured over accounts in poor light in the back room. Credits and debits. Profit and loss. He kept close track of everything. How much water was added to the carafe wine before it was served. How much bread in the mince. Not too many tomatoes in the salad bowl. And how to pass off spiced chicken for turkey.

'Running a restaurant need talent.' He'd smiled. 'When the authorities come in to check on you, you must know how to be nice to them. Stand them a glass of your best wine. With no water in it. Offer them a good meal. They must be starving. Still working at this time of the day. Lay out a special meal for them in the back room. With one of the better looking waitresses to see to their needs. And then, discreetly slip them a sealed envelope. It always works.'

It always had worked for him. Business, it seems, was thriving. His wife went about loaded with ugly but expensive jewellery all times of the day. His son, a spoilt bastard who never did a stroke of work, nor even pretended to be studying at least, much to his father's chagrin, revved up his own sports car after skidding to some ostentatious halt.

'You see? Ungrateful sons-of-bitches. The pair of them. My wife would still be washing dishes from dawn to midnight if it wasn't for me. My son would be up at the crack of dawn, sweating over a lathe if he was lucky. And yet look at them. Sons-of-bitches. I give them everything. Everything and more. And they turn up their noses at me. Don't want to be seen in public with me. Neither of them . . .'

He'd sometimes moan over a strong glass of port, late at night, before closing up.

He took hold of her hand as she passed him while she was clearing up for the night. He caught hold of her hand.

'Be nice to me,' he said. 'Please.'

The young man burst into the kitchen in a pair of tight jeans, distinctly faded over the bulge between his legs. An expensive but vulgar shirt unbuttoned to the waist to reveal a muscular, hairy chest and a thick, gold chain around his neck to match an equally weighty gold bracelet. He grabbed a piece of chicken from the plate she was preparing to serve.

'Old man not here?' he asked, munching noisily, as she despaired quietly over the ruined order.

'As you can see,' she answered in restrained annoyance.

'Bloody old fool. Never there when you need him.'

'He won't be long. He's just popped out to the bank, I think. If you'd like to wait.'

'Bank? For a withdrawal or a deposit?'

'I wouldn't know.' She answered impatiently and turned to make up a new plate for the ruined order.

'Hey, wait a minute.' He stopped her physically, impetuously taking hold of her arm in a rather rough gesture. 'Hey, wait a minute. That's no way to treat the boss's son. I could get you fired, you know.' He sounded extremely proud of his power over her as he said so. 'New here, aren't you? The old man screw you?'

'Leave me alone.' She shook off his arm in disgust.

'Because if he doesn't, I wouldn't mind breaking you in myself. It'd be kind of fun. Bet you're a virgin. They're all virgins from back home when they're new here.' And he laughed with delight as she escaped quickly into the dining room, even without the order he'd just gone and ruined.

The proprietor frowned.

'Money, money. All they ever want from me is money!' he muttered after his son had gone. 'Never done an honest day's work in his life. Never once got up in the morning because he had to. Irresponsible layabout!' he complained. 'When I was his age, I had no time for fun. No time for life. Only work, work, work. I never enjoyed myself, ever!' But he never told him all this to his face. Just quietly, or noisily, lamented over it behind his back. He never told him he should work or even tried to assign anything to him.

'He'd only ruin everything I've toiled so hard to build up,' was his excuse. And he knew it was only an excuse. 'When I was his age, I never had any fun. Let him, at least, enjoy life now that he can.' He confessed, sometimes, when he'd just done the accounts and seemed happy over them. 'He's a young man, after all. Must sow his wild oats.' Then he'd sigh and lapse into nostalgia. 'Had I only had his good luck. There was a girl. From our country too. A wonderful girl. But she wouldn't have me. Married a lawyer instead. Can't say that I blame her.' And another sad sigh before he poured himself a stout port from the bottle he kept just for himself. It was, he shyly admitted, his one and only luxury in life.

'Come for a drive with me, brown eyes,' the son hissed in her ear from behind, startling her dangerously as she set out the glasses and bottles for the order she was getting ready to serve. 'It's your afternoon off today, isn't it?' He grinned in boyish triumph at her expression of surprise mingled with apprehension as she turned round towards him. 'See? How I know these things? I make it my business to know when I've the hots on for someone. I'll pick you up here at five and take you for a spin in the car.' He looked at her confused, speechless expression and added with a leer of delight, 'You'll love it baby. You'll really love it!' before stealing quickly out of the back door like a thief as he saw his father approaching.

'What did he want?' His face was pale and stern, betraying an unusual nervousness as his mouth twitched. 'What did he want?' he insisted. She'd never seen him so wrought and tense at her before.

'Nothing,' she shrugged.

'That's not true.' He accused her indirectly but surely enough of lying to him.

'I mean.' She felt confused and a bit guilty before him. 'I mean, he wanted nothing from you.'

'That's not what I asked.' His expression as austere as her own father's would have been under the circumstances. 'What did he want?' he repeated. 'No lies.'

She lowered her eyes, feeling strangely compelled by his manner, and told him. In any case, she admitted, she wouldn't have gone for the drive. No offence meant to him or his son, and she was grateful indeed for this job and under no circumstances did she wish to lose it, but she really didn't want to go for the drive with him anyway. She asked him to understand. And he seemed to. In fact more than she realised herself. He smiled, patted her shoulder warmly and told her he'd tell his son to leave her alone. She should look on him like a father. She shouldn't be afraid. She should tell him everything and he'd be there to protect her. He smiled broadly, delight beaming from his features as he whistled happily when he turned to go back to the kitchen.

A cold, stormy evening. Not much business that day because of the weather. The rain came down in torrents beating noisily against the window panes. His mood was bad. Choice Dover sole wasted. The succulent roast beef would have to go into tomorrow's cold plate. Overall, a bad evening. His wife had lost at gin rummy again and junior had disappeared for a week only bothering to phone his mother once to tell her he loved only her. A prelude, as always, to get her to intercede for more money when father thought he was being adamant in his refusal to fork out any more.

'He's only a boy.' She ventured hesitantly to help cool his seething temper and not out of any softness for the young man himself whom she'd begun to abhor, especially after all the horrible things he'd said to her when it had become clear she wouldn't go with him.

'Shut up!' He spoke to her angrily and rudely, in a manner he'd never used with her before. 'Don't stick up for that bastard. I don't even know if he's mine.'

She couldn't help gaping at the unexpected admission and wondering if there might be any truth in it.

'What are you looking at me like that for?' he snapped disagreeably. 'You think I don't know? You think when I spend all my life in this smelly, steamy kitchen from dawn to dawn and sleep in my bed only three hours a night that I don't know?' He screamed out as though it were her fault. 'You think I don't know I waste my time toiling, fretting, losing my life for an ungrateful woman and a bastard who's not even mine!'

'I really don't think . . . ' She ventured again, but he cut her off sharply with another fuming, raging, angered.

'Shut up!' And then he cried over his glass of port. His only extravagance in life. His only solace. A glass of stout, vintage port from the expensive bottle he kept for himself.

It was a cold, harsh winter, especially for her, unused as she was to such low temperatures, the fog and, above all, the loneliness. A damp, empty room with no one there to return to. A room so cold and so un-welcoming for being totally deserted so many hours during the day. From early morning to late at night. A cold, unfriendly room, with a shared bathroom and kitchenette, but no one to talk to. The other tenants were as busy as she and her hours, in any case, were not suited to socialising. Her afternoons off, she spent mostly sleeping. It was a tiring job. A harsh, cruel winter. Was it really worth all this hardship for a steady job and good wages? At least he didn't cheat on her over-time. And at home, there were so many months to feed and work scarce when not in fact totally non-existent.

'I'm your employer,' he'd said. 'It's in your interest to be nice to me. Respect me. Treat me with the respect you would have for your own father. Do my bidding as you would his. Don't forget. I can get your permit withdrawn and have you deported any time. So think carefully before you decide.'

His threats had been clear and obvious. A corpulent, middle-aged man with a pencil stuck behind his ear as he sat in his shirt sleeves, his tie hanging loose round his neck, doing his accounts in the half light of the back room.

'It takes talent to run a restaurant like this. Talent.' He took pride in his achievement.

He held onto her hand tightly. The hand he had clutched at as she passed him, clearing things up for the night. It was a cold stormy night. The rain pelted noisily and heavily against the window pane. It had been a bad evening for business.

'Be nice to me,' he'd muttered tensely. Then added a strange, almost incongruent after all those threats, 'Please.'

And in the end it wasn't the threats, which she knew very well he wouldn't carry out, even before she got him to admit as much to her before she committed herself. And it wasn't the newly mellowed hints that he hoped there'd be more in it for her too. Something positive. Not just negative. Something more substantial than pleasure, which he hoped he would manage to give her. He sounded strangely abashed and shyly hesitant over that part of it. And not even the final promise of getting her a warm, decent,. self contained little flat, much as she could do with just that too.

Alone, in the large, empty restaurant on a stormy night after a bad day for business. She sat with him for the first time in the back room where he kept his accounts and took the sip that was offered from his glass of port. It was too strong for her. She grimaced. He looked at her searchingly, awaiting her answer. The rain pelted down on the windows. The lighted flickered, the power, no doubt, being affected by the storm raging outside.

She stretched her hand out in the silence and rested it gently on his face. Slightly hesitantly, slightly cautiously, she rested her hand on his rough cheek and caressed him.

'You're such an unhappy man,' she whispered.

But it wasn't out of pity either, nor even the overwhelming desire to bury herself in the arms of a fellow human being, cuddle close to him for the warmth of his body and soul on a cold, lonely night in a foreign, unfriendly country. Perhaps it was something of all of these.

Or perhaps it was just the way he'd said, 'Please.'

Stephen Spender

POÈTES MAUDITS

I

Under the X-ray sun, two *poètes*
Maudits sit drinking absinthe: *Paul*
Lecherously lachrymose at having
Abandoned wife, child, priest, for *Rhim*
Heaven-born boy with Hell-fire tongue,
Hair a black halo round his head,
Dark eyes that stare into his fate.

Drunken on language, they hurl down
In rivalry between them, boasts,
Each clamouring he had the more
Obscene childhood, spent all day
Crouching in holes of closets, spying
Up at those parts the grown-ups hide
Under dense hypocrisies
Of hymns sung, sermons preached, in church:
Cocks cunts arse-holes from out of whose
Passages issue piss shit blood
Excremental extremities
Dictionaries grudge four letters to
And doctors bury in deep tomes
Of dead words in dead languages
The labels of those Latin names.

Delirious with the ecstasy
Of shames let fly against the sun
Rhim leaps up on the table, tears
His clothes apart above the knees
And shows embossed upon one thigh
A cicatrice like a medallion.
'My gilded stamp of sin,' he cries
'That I was born with, my true self
'Under heaven's hypocrisies.'

Ecstatic at such innocence
Of shames let fly against the sun
Paul, slobbering, rises from his chair
And plants his tongue upon that place.

White with contempt, the boy taunts him:
'Mad aunt! Crazed shepherdess! Be off!'
And knocks *Paul* down. *Paul* rises, feels
Inside the darkness of a pocket
A gun that yearns to reach its target,
Rhim's ice-black heart, the centre of
Their love turned hate: aiming at
That centre, misses – wounds a finger.

The boy, become all child again,
Runs to his mother's womb – 'Police! Help!
Maman!' Two gendarmes, rushing in
Take *Paul* away, to spend two years
Bleeding poems that are penances.

II

Rhim rushes from the café, walks
With scissor strides past fields hills towns
All day, and all night, sleepless, reads,
Written across the dark his one
True poem true world his childhood when,
At cock-crow, from his parents' house,
He saw rainbows of dew cling to
Threads spiders wove between grass blades
Near meadows where hares raced, with thudding
Jack-in-the-box hind legs that struck
The new day's surface like a drum,
While from low cottages small children
Ran out and danced in jeering rings
Round steeples of their kneeling mothers.

Strode on and on till he reached Paris
That earliest hour when light and dark
Are ghosts laid in each other's arms
Merged within one gray monochrome,
And the gray houses their own tombs:

Then street cleaners came out to hose
Down avenues; and, in shirt sleeves,
Waiters to tables on the street
To throw out drunks through whose gross heads
Last night's brawls still reverberated.

Then shutters of shop windows rose
Upon the theatre of the day
Traffic and people –

               Rhim strides past
The pavement where he sees himself
The boy two years ago who fled
From his home begging shelter from –
Maker of poems that he most loved –
Paul, who received him as a god

And showed him off to drugged Parnassians
And took to salons of princesses:
Debauched boy genius from his village
With that wild look of being struck
By tempests of the world his time
That penetrated through his senses
Into his innermost self and proved
In words the birth of a new love.

And yet some primal thing in him
The pagan slave the peasant stock
Made him detest them; the princesses
The writers of the *feuilletons*

But most the poets their curling beards
Their agate eyes their public hearts
Their poetry with its senile tears
The paper-thin *vie litteraire*

That bumph he left behind and strode
From Paris, whore of whores, to meet
Through brazen gates the modern world.

III

   London –Milan – Stuttgart – Vienna–
By legs – trains – ships –

From Hardewijk on the Zuyder Zee
Conscript of the Dutch Colonial army –

On the *Prinz van Oranje*

– Skipped ship at Samarang –
Jungles of Java – natives –

Worked his way back –
Bremen Stockholm Copenhagen –

Foreman of Mazeran-Vianay-Bardeygang
Construction workers –
Cypriots, Greeks, Syrians –

   The sky a lottery from which
He drew a fiery ticket –
Africa! – Hurrah! – Harar!
Director of the Agence Pinchard –

                   *   *   *

   Remains, one photograph of *Rhim*
White-suited stiff-haired bronzed
A lone explorer's face among
Sacks of coffee beans — and heaps
Of skins of desert prey — and bottles —
Account books — ledgers —

Dreaming of mapping Zanzibar

                   *   *   *

   (O, Capitalism,
The poetry of the real —
Captains of factories
Explorers engineers inventors —
Brains of diamond hearts of steel —

The globe's material from which
They make their artefacts
   — Canals

Cut through isthmuses
So two converging seas may kiss
   — And laying railways down
Across the continents like arms
Of populations till then apart
Meeting between mountain chains
On plains and valleys, their love beds.

A Version of Melancholy

It can come in several forms, no matter where you live. Particularly in this city, Cape Town, it is November that usually brings the worst of it. You wake one morning and sense at once the vacuum in the atmospheric pressure: overnight the winds have swung around from north to south to begin their summer-long blowing. These south-easters, rainless, relentless, can air-blast the city for five days and nights at a stretch, until they seem less a part of local weather, only to be expected at this time of the year, and more nature's way of having a nervous breakdown. They can blow until they shift the day slightly off-centre, become something metaphysical, enlarging nothingness. They bring with them the perennial refuse, the newsprint that wraps itself around lamp-posts and is torn to shreds by its paroxysms of vain flapping. Under their gritty scouring all surfaces become more surface-like, dry as dry pumice stone, raspingly abrasive. Parked cars shiver on their sets of suspension; the curl of leaves grows bruised, wind-bitten. Now the sea just beyond the harbour breakwater turns the blackened green of a sewage farm. All too soon along the many sections of unpaved, suburban pavement, scabs of dead, grey sand appear; the riff-raff of winter weed dries out, turns to thorn. On the mountain flanks pits of gravel, like sores, open up and erode in smudges of orange dust. From other patches of raw earth and construction sites beside major roads, an incessant stream of runaway dust and builder's sand skids across the tar. This wind diminishes every-thing, brings things to a point where an entire city's three-centuries toehold on the African continent seems about to slip and slide, in one final blast, into the adjacent sea. It brings with it that feeling.

You have only to go down to what is called the 'foreshore' of the city to experience it afresh. There, already, the light will be infected by the vacancy of the open-ended boulevard on which it does not cease to pour. Caught up in all that flying air, it too will have been rubbed thin, eroded. In the absence of louring cloud or densely wooded horizons, all else will have been reduced to something somehow dispersed, vacant, the human beings themselves wrought to stick-figures, the blue of the sky faded as a piece of stretched, perished balloon, your own heart a vessel, empty, without resonance. Should you go out to the Cape Flats in such weather, to that hinge of land, sheeted with marine sand, that joins the city's peninsula to the rest of Africa, the southeaster will be harder still, that much more riddled by sand. The Hottentots Holland mountains, our barrier range, will be too far off to staunch the emptiness of sky. Seeing these waste lands full of wattle, dead weed, molehills, still flat as the ocean bed of which they formed a part aeons ago, then finding that further vacancy that opens up just beyond the city's acreage of level suburban roofs, you will be forced back once more into something that goes far beyond the obvious reaction: 'What a dump!' You will in fact be encountering a version of our melancholy, a cultural experience not to be found in most local books, films, theatre productions, never ever referred to in political circles, but nevertheless one which is probably more central to South African life, and an understanding of that life, than any other.

Antoine Roquentin in Sartre's *Nausea* experienced the absurdity of existence in the bloated roots of a chestnut tree, in the fatness and meaningless proliferation of organic matter. Universal as his disgust might have been, in its implications at least, his reaction was more First World than Third World. The viscid is more the province of Europe; it takes a great deal of history to produce it. We have our nausea too, but it issues from something other than the lubricity of nature. In South Africa it is much more the thinness rather than the mindless coagulation of matter that afflicts. Here, it is the thread-bareness, the extempore character of almost all man-made structures, the loose warp and woof of all textures, natural or cultural, that underscores the absurdity of our projects, existential or otherwise. This thinness is at the basis of whatever metaphysic we possess. One could write a treatise on its presence, year-in, year-out, in skies immo-bilized by their own vacancy, lands drugged by their own distances, the many South African dusks, diluted, the colour of barley-water. And in these, as in all other cases, it would return one to that thinnest of feelings in the spectrum of emotions, that melancholy.

No account of the syndrome would be complete without reference to the expatriate South African novelist, Dan Jacobson. What he wrote of the country several decades ago is still true of the place as a whole:

the social fabric [in South Africa] has a thinness, a simplicity, a tenuousness which it is diffi-cult to describe, but which one must include in any enumeration of the conditions governing intellectual life in the country. It is this condition which I have called the *absence of established and highly developed social forms* . . . The social tenuousness, the paucity of accepted social usages, is not something absctract, remote from one's everyday perception of the life around one. It might seem an exaggeration to say that one can hear an echo of it in the South African voice and accent, see a reflection of it even in the South African face; but in fact it is no exag-geration at all. And to think of this is to be reminded too of what I would call the imaginative flatness of the country's streets, of its buildings, even of its landscapes which seem merely to have been scratched or eroded, not developed and moulded, by the people who live among them.

There is, in a sense, nothing superficial about this superficiality. It can impress itself on a writer's imagination with as much force as any of the particular social and political torments of the country. Another quotation from an essay of his, first published in the 1960s:

my single overwhelming impression of South Africa when I look back now, is not political. What I chiefly remember of the country are its spaces, simply; all the empty unused land-scapes of a country that still seems to lie bereft of any human past, untouched by its own history. Blue sky, brown earth, and people who live unaccommodated between: that is the abiding image of South Africa. There is something remote, far-sunken about the country, dwarfing the people who live in it, and making them, in turn, seem remote from one another.

Perhaps more than any other single writer, Jacobson has been able to convey the degree to which many a South African life has been afflicted by a version of homelessness almost transcendental in its intensity. Time and time again his early work reveals the extent to which South Africans of all complexions have either lost or been fated never to know a harmonious, integrated connection with their world. They recognize their contemporary isolation, repeatedly long for the archetypal connections and cultural roots of tradition, without which there is no psychic wholeness. And yet equally often they are forced by the very character of the country itself to forego any myth of home-coming (which is probably the most powerful governing myth in all South African literature), to remain strangers in this world, little more than probationer exiles, emotionally homeless as the central character in Jacobson's early novella, *A Dance in the Sun* (1956):

It was a kind of homesickness, I felt then, but it was a sickness for a home I had never had, for a single cultivated scene, for a country less empty and violent, for people whose manners and skins and languages were fitted peaceably together. The lorry on which we had hitched a lift from that young couple, whose little history I had just heard, had hurled us towards the man next to whom I stood, and whom I had never seen before, across endless countrysides of heat-seized, silent veld . . . a multi-tongued nation of nomads we seemed to be, across a country too big and silent for us, too dry for cultivation, about which we went on roads like chains. We were caught within it, within this wide, sad land we mined but did not cultivate.

A version of melancholy.

Nothing could be more trivial than to suggest that this syndrome, with all its depressing, depressive effects, is simply a consequence of politics – apartheid specifically. In point of fact, it preceded apartheid by many years and, given all the economic indices, all the demo-gragraphic factors with their logic of future catastrophe, is certain to outlast the demise of institutionalized racism. It is no doubt true that Dan Jacobson, like many another South African writer, has been a member of a white English-speaking sub-culture which has, since the Afrikaner Nationalist victory at the polls in 1948, been afflicted by a loss of control, of powerlessness paradoxical in a group which has so effortlessly dictated the course of the country's economic develop-ment. More recent expatriates, most especially the novelist Christopher Hope in his South African travelogue, *White Boy Running* (1988), have given vivid expression to a politics of melan-choly, to that impotence experienced by those of liberal inclinations caught, in South Africa, in the no-man's-land of vehement, com-peting nationalisms. Theirs is the melancholia of the inner émigré, of those who know they have lost and will always lose in the battle to shape the kind of South Africa they would prefer to live in. And yet one has only to think of the widespread decimation of indigenous cultures, the urbanization of the Afrikaners, the makeshift (the piece-meal, the patchwork) that reigns in almost all spheres of life, the pro-found, deadening depths of triviality evident in the quality of the daily press (in which, tirelessly, members of the human species disport themselves in 'steamy sex romps'), and then the inroads made by commercial American culture, to realize that this thinness of culture and its melancholic effects are not just the perception of a certain minority of marginalized writers, projecting from an acute sense of political dispossession. Even if this was the case, the truth of what they have perceived – this dessication that lives on – is verified by the pain that its recognition constantly involves.

The phenomenon knows no distinctions of class. It is there in con-sumerist aspirations of lower middle-class blacks and whites, in the characteristic merchandise of the stores that serve them: lounge suites covered in button-down tartan terry-cloth, in moulded plastic garden-furniture, varnished pine beds with floral foam-rubber mattresses. It is present in the multitude of lives straitened by hire-purchase terms, whose days amount to anything but the repeated fulfilment of the pleasure principle, whose lives are confined to the strict but unspoken limits of an income bracket never high enough for the achievement of beauty or the discriminations of taste. It grows chronic in all one's encounters with the décor, fabricated or prefabricated, of families absolutely nuclear, who have just had another child, who in this era of sanctions and steady economic decline are forever struggling to 'make ends meet', who can just afford a new braai on wheels, who need a col-lapsible corduroy-covered sofa-bed for an aged relative who has come to stay. To the outsider there is a pathos almost awe-inspiring in the efforts of this class in the direction of transcendence or self-improvement: the girl teenager pirouetting in her tutu on the stoep; the copper geese in their crucified flight up an otherwise naked lounge wall; the budgie's cage near the sofa; the piano against the net curtain that has the appearance of a giant doily. Common domestic icons like these are no cause for condescension, snobbery, or mockery. They define the true conditions in which a multitude of people make their lives in this country. They make for a world in which there is not a

trace of eroticism, in which attepts at style, at an idea of life as pleasure, even joy, home as a place of comfort, seem long since to have
gone awry.

But there is something equally, if less obviously sad in the characteristic middle-class milieu. For even the rich in South Africa are
more often *nouveau riche* than rich. In their endless 'showhouses', in
the new shopping-malls they frequent, tiled with imported Italian
marble, banistered with blonde Scandinavian woods, the boutiques
as international as certain brands of cigarettes, the evidence of wealth
remains that much more artificial, as if only recently excavated, raw as
the new mined ore on which so much of it is ultimately based. In a
city like Johannesburg particularly, there is an almost ludicrous dis-
proportion between this class's conspicuous skill in extracting surplus
value and its equally evident cultural subsistence economy. And there
persists the element of plain parody. In the expensive fashions on the
expensive women, their class hardened in high cheekbones and eyes
used to reproaching servants, an idea of Europe continues to be played
out. But in one way or another the streets here are always just a little
too wide, the buildings never quite old enough, the light simply too
corrosive for such imitations to be sustained. Just beyond the neatly-
bricked car park of the shrine to Europe, the African sun continues to
pulverise itself in the orange dirt, the coarse frost-parched grass and
all the surplus mess of nature begins. Just around the corner, cigarette
butts and bottle-tops litter the hot dead sand surrounding a bus stop;
that wind begins once more. As the imported, patent-leather Italian
shoes clip-clop past, by now more an expression of cultural helpless-
ness than status symbol or expression of plain white greed, one
wonders what could possibly make it cohere, this culture of the hodge-
podge. The maize-meal soufflé of it all.

Above all, it is when one first sees the work of the photographer
David Goldblatt – unquestionably South Africa's most eminent and
one of the truly important artists working in any medium in this
country today – that one realizes that the syndrome, whatever its
various manifestations, is pre-political as the flue virus, but no less
prepotent for being that. His photographs, especially those collected

in *Some Afrikaners Photographed* (1975) and later in *In Boksburg* (1982), gives new definition, even paradoxical depth, to a word often used of South African culture in general – 'shallow'. They reveal as nothing else before them the very textures of experience in this country, and with so great a degree of attention that it is these textures themselves – the Orlons, Perlons, Nylons and Crimplenes of the great mass of South African lives – that become as representative as any of the more obvious cultural icons. In fact, in a good many of Goldblatt's suburban lanscapes and interiors, documenting the surfaces amongst which many lives pass, history itself becomes a texture: it is inscribed in the linoleum on a Boksburg floor; in the fall-out of black shale across a Karoo plain; in the grain of a tarred car-park outside a dis- count store. His work as a whole goes to show that there is as much, if not more, evidence of the condition of a culture in a study of a Vibra- crete wall – in the malady of its fake-brick texture – as there might be in the action shot of someone hurling a brick. Like very few others before him, he strikes one as actually having *looked* at the evidence of South African lives; the juxtapositions of new concrete and raw sun- light out-of-doors, dull rubber house-plants in dull plastic tubs indoors, the sound of Hoovers in the deadened time of mid-morning almost palpable in the silence. So steady is his gaze that such objects such surfaces, are revealed not only in the poverty of their design, but an entire culture starts dissolving, is reduced to a basic, seemingly primordial nakedness, to the vacancy inherent in such things.

David Goldblatt's world, particularly as portrayed in works like *In Boksburg*, is predominantly a Highveld, Transvaal one. But it is also ubiquitous, at least so far as South Africa is concerned. The Trans- vaal might have a veritable lexicon of melancholy in those place names extending eastwards from Johannesburg: in Bocksburg, Benoni, Brak- pan, Springs – all the way to Ogies. But Cape Town has its own in that drab declension of suburbs going north from the city itself: Goor- wood, Parow, Bellville, Brackenfell, even farther than the far and tree- less Peerless Park in Kraaifontein. There is, in any case, no regional variation in the standardized designs and produce of the major stores, nor in the smaller ones with their window signs accepting 'lay-byes', their coconut-shy pyramids of canned fruit on 'specials', the dishwashing fluid discounted that week, the nesting sets of aluminium saucepans, the schoolchildren's cardboard satchels coloured in imitation of leather, the virulently synthetic orange of plastic lunch-boxes. North and south, such things are all an indelible part of our true national culture, and, in one way or another, Goldblatt captures their universality.

He is, in fact, one of the finest cultural historians we possess. Throughout his work, whatever its conceptual and other brilliances, it is the surfaces – the grains, the patinas, the textures – that are seen in stark relief: the light flattened on concrete pavings, absolutely symmetrical, burning in the heat of the day: the tarmac detailed by oil stains, gobs of discarded chewing-gum, the sugary black patches of spilt cool-drinks, smears of old dog-turd; the ersatz pile of the cheaper varieties of wall-to-wall carpeting and other household totems that attest more to the poverty of human desires than to their vanity. He forces the viewer to contemplate one surface after another, until a kind of vacuity opens up in the compositions themselves. There is, they seem to suggest, nothing beyond themselves, nothing beneath them. This is a culture, it is implied, that is as deep as its pandemic linoleum. And more conclusively than any verbal, rhetorical statements, images like these declare that God is dead, history evidently the same, the great white psyche a punctured squash-box.

In photographs like 'A girl and her mother at home', 'Showhouse near completion at Parkrand' or 'Saturday Afternoon in Sunward Park', he depicts a cultural world which is not so much beyond good and evil as beneath it. In focusing on so many surfaces, another kind of emptiness – a moral emptiness – begins to declare itself. Nothing in this man-made, woman-made world, such is the suggestion, betrays the degree of consciousness which might make conscience possible. Of Goldblatt's work Lionel Abrahams has written: 'His awareness goes far and subtly beyond the notorious features of our society, into the textures and range of experience.' But in fact it goes still further. In his photographs it is almost never the sight of riot policemen, tear-gas cannisters smoking, chanting or fleeing crowds, that is shown to be emblematic or symptomatic of a vicious, bankrupt social order. Rather, it is these surfaces, frozen in silence, impenetrable in their

blandness, that are revealed as insidious. It is the lack of depth or suggestion of depth in the fabrics, in the countless artefacts never
mythologized by time, that becomes as threatening as anything else.
For they all disclose that basic streak of nihilism which is seldom
absent from contemporary South African life, a nihilism whose
malignity has nothing to do with a Satanic denial of God or
Nietzschean pride, but which is insiduous by virtue of its plain emptiness, its passive indifference to all values, its unadulterated, unbudge-
able blankness.

In the face-brick of all the new 'spec-built' houses of the country's
Sunward Parks, roughcast to simulate a patina of the natural, the
rustic, history evaporates. In the new estates he photographs, where
piles of builder's rubble still abound and there are as yet no trees
around the fake sapphires of chlorinated swimming-pools, time is
paralysed. In the façades of numberless houses, bungalow-style,
neither brazen nor abashed, their roofs neatly horizontal against a
neat, hygienic sky, a mediocrity continues to reign with all the con-
sistency of mediocrity. Light pours down unstintingly, but nowhere on
a culture even coherently pagan in its love of light. Governments
might come and go, social orders be overturned and replaced, but the
faces will live on in their physiology of vacancy, in lives that know no
transcendent possibility. At the end of a thousand lawns, dying in the
heat or burnt beige by cold, nature will continue to sprawl, as if it too
had been pulled through a bush backwards. Above the main streets of
another thousand country dorps, isolated in their perpetual Sunday-
afternoon ennui, the same South African sky will continue to be canti-
levered by its unflawed blue into a further nothingness – an infinity
like nothingness. All the signs, like Goldblatt's masterly photographs
themselves, will reveal how far a distance has to be travelled before
this country, in its entirety, achieves truly significant cultural change.

Indeed, there is no escaping it, however much you might dream of
flight. Even if you take the road north from Cape Town, the land just
beyond the mountain pass soon lapses into sameness, the plains are
mantras, endlessly repeating themselves, addled by that sameness.
Just off the shoulders of the national road, the raggedness begins

again: an eventless plateau starts rising while, farther off, mountains
float once more, hot and grey, against the sky. Immaterial as the blue
above, now without moisture, powdery to look at, they travel with you
all the way to Beaufort West, like the veld itself with its littering of
shale, exactly the rusted, dead colour of the chipped stone that forms
the bed of the north-bound railway-line. Out here there is not a trace
of southeaster wind; no breeze tunes itself in the slack ellipses of
telephone-wires spanning the country. There are no suburbs nor sign,
even, of those one-star platteland hotels with their 'ladies lounges' and
district postmasters who get drunk every day out of a grief at a human
project that seems all in vain.

Stopping for a while in the midst of nowhere, you could even
believe it was all an illusion, that melancholy and its variations, no
more than a premonitory sign in you of an entire country's descent
into Third-World status, an economic process through which it is sure
to be Africanized more fully than through any conscious political pro-
gramme. But you have only to delay a little longer to realize that here
too, in your mind, in the landscape, or somewhere in between, it lives
on. It has something to do with those mountains, pale as unfired
pottery, growing duller, more immaterial still, as the light fails. It has
something to do with these plains, daubed with the heads of small
bushes, still black under all that sunlight. And also because there is too
much dust out here for hope, perhaps too much vacancy for love.

But whether it is the result of a white culture that once sold its col-
lective soul for gold and is still determined not to find it, whether it is
embodied in the photographs of David Goldblatt or illuminated by the
words of Dan Jacobson and others, it is still there. It persists as the
basis of whatever national culture we have, part of the true material
conditions of that culture, limiting whatever future culture is conceivable. It is multi-racial, plural, non-sexist – our one common
denominator. No words, no fists, can do more than prevail against it.
This most telling of local cultural experiences will continue to
manifest itself years hence. And whatever the form it might take,
whatever the dismay its re-appearance might arouse, it comes time
and time over to take each one of us back, alone, to the inalienable,
parched sources of our South African existence.

Jack Mapanje

THESE STRAGGLING MUDHUTS OF KIRK RANGE
(For Brown & George, 1991)

Four years ago a battered initiate
Staggered out of those grass-huts
From a contraption of stunted weed,

Torn cartoons and witch-oil-black
Cardboards held together by split
Bamboo and cords of bark; and trapped

In the heat between these hostile
Boulders and the misty valleys of
Villa Ulongue, she nervously peered

Into the tarmac of our makeshift
Borders, her wind-blown babe suckling
The bitter sweat of her dry breasts,

Her teeth (tartarred by wild fruit
On flight) exposing embittered memories
Of yet another home charred, goats,

Ducks and chicks scattered by shrapnel
From the enemy: her own people. But
Today, from these sprawling mud-shacks

Permanently huddled below Kirk Range
And sometimes threatening to leap like
Sand-frogs in the rain but beaten back

Squatting like grey turtles stuck
Between Inkosi Gomani's dwindling grave
And the tarmac road; today, from this

Straggling shackscape a chaperon and
A boy defiantly declare their UNHCR
Wares beside the highway: tins of butter

From European Community mountains,
Paraffin glass lanterns from Mozambique
And gallons of American cooking oil

(Bartering for the much needed dry fish
The donors overlooked). Today, the mother
Even manages a bleak joke about her son's

Father who slunk back home to smuggle
What remained behind of his own but never
Came back! But watch this woman tomorrow;

After the Berlin Wall, watch the trump
She mothers in this triangular struggle
For these crusty boulders. And she is

Not oblivious of the sand shifting underfoot nor those multipartisms embarrassing
These starved implacable borders! Watch.

WHERE DISSENT IS MEAT FOR CROCODILES
(A Martyr's Day History, March 3, 1992)

Since the cyclone domina first
Lashed out its tail on those sanjika
Brimful dug-outs, since the first
Revolt at the nation's conception,
This monster of state we openly hope

To tame, regardless, continues rest-
lessly to breed its plethora of
Baffling metaphors benumbing even
The children. But this beast is vile;
It has persistently, blatantly wrung
And squelched nimble necks of sparrows
And hanging them tight between sharp
Split bamboos for the universe to
Watch and mock, dangled them in the sun
Until the last drop of truth has
Fallen. This beast we seek to acquit
And confirm has poisoned the crown
Of the rhino's horn without tears
Or shame; the very falcon has failed
To perch on those mango branches for
Prey. What of the blood of protesting
Students and starving workers? What
Of cudgelling to death these helpless
Mortals bailing out women wearing
Trousers at jando (that circumcision
Right for boys)? Today, his dossier
Thickens with more, clotting, stodgy
Figures, some that still bloodily flow
Unabated. And you brethren in dissent
Are out of bounds, meat for crocodiles,
Mere cliché in our country's anthology
Of martyrs, perhaps even smudges on
The blank page of this nation and our
Tyrant's boast of crocodile images
Of power. But in a century crying out
For love, what rancorous metaphors!

Letters from England or on English Art

To Monsieur PIERRET,
   rue de l'Université, No.46 Faubourg Saint-Germain, Paris.

London, Sunday May 27th 1825

Messieurs Guillemardet and Pierret
   To both of them.

My address is: 14, Charles Street, Middlesex Hospital.

My dear child,
   I have already spent two or three days in this great city and scarcely had time to write to you, so weary am I still after my travels which, however, were very satisfactory. The mail coach is a means of travel which I find most pleasant. Besides, I was fortunate in having to deal with a good fellow who was helpful to me in all sorts of ways. I reached Calais at half-past ten in the evening, leaving it again the next morning, a Thursday, at half-past ten to reach Dover at half-past twelve or one o'clock in the afternoon, after having been much shaken by the crossing, but without any sea-sickness, which pleased me no end, though I had relied on sea-sickness as a cure for my cold; it would have served as a little treatment of enforced vomiting to rid me of my ill, with which I'm still afflicted, though not as badly as before. In Dover, I found time to climb the cliffs which Copley Fielding painted in a lovely water-colour which you surely remember; I also saw the Castle that dominates the harbour.
   My first steps in England nevertheless failed to delight me. I was extremely impatient to enter the harbour. As soon as I landed, I felt

little sympathy for all that I saw, an impression which has lasted indeed until now. Especially after reaching London, I have felt constantly that I would find myself most unhappy here, were I obliged to stay forever. Yet I am, by nature, somewhat of a cosmopolitan. But I have an idea that what has so far shocked me here may have done this because of my lack of experience of English customs. Quite naturally, I compared all that I saw with French usages, and loved all of you all the more for these. In fact, I was feeling real hostility to my new surroundings.

In the mail-coach from Dover to London, I found an elderly Frenchman of some merit and we both enjoyed speaking ill of England in the presence of a stout *goddam* of an Englishman who, in truth, understood not a word of what we were saying, first for lack of any knowledge of French, then too because of two bottles of port-wine which he saw fit to obtain before leaving Dover in order to fortify himself against the boredom of the road. This presentation indeed made him wildly cheerful whenever he was not snoring.

The vastness of this city cannot well be conceived. The bridges across the river are built so far apart that, from any one of them, one can scarcely see the next one. What shocked me most was the lack of anything that we might call architecture. Whether I'm prejudiced or not, I find this displeasing. And then, they have here a Waterloo Road which is just lined with opera-palaces, one after another and all leading up to an edifice with a bell-tower just like this [Delacroix includes here a sketch]. It's ghastly.

But what beautiful shops! What extreme luxury! The daylight too is here of a special kind, always as on the day of a solar eclipse. I've already seen a lot of London in a very short while. Yesterday, I went with six young friends, including the Fielding brothers, to Richmond, by water on the Thames. To get there, we covered some six leagues or more in two and a half hours, and the same on the way back, in a boat with six oars, which is worth the trip from Paris as a sight in itself; imagine an Amati violin, as delicate as anything conceivable, the most extraordinary thing that I have so far seen in this country. I cannot tell you how admirable it is. I was granted the honour of holding the rudder. The banks of the Thames are charming and I recognized there all the landscapes that Soulier is constantly painting.

I also went to a show, a play called *Napoleon's Invasion of Russia*. It's very funny. They've managed to imitate very well the main character, who begins all his speeches to his brave soldiers by addressing them as 'Gentlemen'! But how comical are these unfortunate soldiers! Their uniforms, for instance, are a tangle of droll mistakes. All this was in a theatre like Franconi's, with horses on the stage. The English are very expert at this kind of spectacle.

Fielding had reserved me very suitable lodgings that cost me scarcely forty francs a month, which is very cheap, isn't it? It turns out, however, not to be true that *goddam* is the very basis of the English language. *One shilling, sir*, comes closer to the facts. It means: *Un schelling, Monsieur*, and turns up at the end of every sentence. I'm not speaking here of conversations held in the Royal Palace, but I have not yet had an opportunity to overhear any conversation of that quality.

I visited Mr West's gallery, for a shilling, of course. There's a lot that can be said about it, as indeed about everything. We'll discuss it together. Now, I'll content myself with embracing you both. I expect I'll write to Edouard tonight, urging him to join me here, if possible. Remind me, please, to all who are dear to both of you and to me too, for this reason.

Your friend,

E. Delacroix.

To SOULIER
London, this June 6th 1825

I'm at last in this country that is almost your home and where I regret very much not having you near me. It is impossible to find oneself better received, with a more nobly generous courtesy than I have encountered among the persons to whom I happened to be recommended. This city is superb and not at all like ours, in many respects. But, when all is said and done, it turns out to be the same kind of life, and I already feel as if I had not moved away from Paris. During the first few days, I was cruelly bored and felt ready to return home without any further ado. This was because I was doing little else than running here and there, with no profit but weariness from all my sightseeing. Since I settled down to work, I've enjoyed being here. I'm very much of a dawdler, to be truthful, but not really an idler in the way that I'll now explain: I'm barely interested in seeing in London a mass of things that are perhaps very curious indeed, but which scarcely fell within my own field of interests, and there are so many curiosities of this kind in Paris which I have never felt any desire to see there so that I'm in no mood to begin leading such a life here. I'm even ready to admit to you that these never-ending galleries of paintings are all very much alike and, if one is familiar with one of them, one knows the others too.

My first contacts with their painting failed to give me pleasure, but I'm now becoming accustomed to it. I'm not surprised by the unfavourable impressions of it that all who do not share our views on these matters bring back to France. The imitation of the old masters, like anything else, has its handicaps.

A Society of persons of great influence is being established here; with the help of the government, it will encourage artists to paint large pictures. I fear that this policy may mean disaster for the English School, which has admirable painters as long as the proportions of their works remain moderate. A desire to attract more attention will make them deviate from the path which they have been following. They'll then paint huge compositions that are no longer within the means of private patrons. This new Society has already purchased a large daub from M. Hilton, for a sum of twenty-five thousand pounds. It's an awkward hodge-podge of memories of everything that the great masters have ever painted. But they also produce there some very beautiful *genre* paintings. I called on Wilkie in his studio and appreciate his work now that I have seen so much of it there. His finished paintings had previously failed to please me; actually, his studies and sketches could never be praised as highly as they deserve. Like all painters of all ages and nations, he regularly spoils his best work. But there is still enough to content one in his counterfeits of his best.

The horses, carriages, side-walks and parks, the Thames, the boats on the Thames, the banks of the Thames, Richmond and Greenwich, the ships, all this would require volumes of letters to describe. We'll discuss it all later, at leisure. This country seems to have been tailor-made to fit your talents. Italy turned your whole shop topsy-turvy. Constantly, I rediscover here those skies, those river-banks, all the effects that appear again and again in your painting.

Fielding is the best of fellows. Copley is a man whom one scarcely sees and who is not much attuned to my own character. The sunshine is not the most brilliant of England's attributes. I have not yet managed to cure myself of a cold that I brought with me from France; this is because the cold weather keeps on returning. I have no idea of how you are faring. If you go to Paris, please remind me *kindly* to your good friends of the rue Saint-Dominique.

Your friend,

E. Delacroix.

Please tell Madame de Ron (Cherolles) that Frenchwomen need fear no equals for their charm.

To J. B. PIERRET, Esqre.
Rue de l'Universite, 46, in Paris.
June 18th 1825.

I am writing to Soulier. Send him the enclosed, after reading it. It's still but a part of the feelings that this country arouses in me. You don't write to me and are probably expecting that London friends will make me forget those I have in Paris. You want me to lose my affection for you, with everything then contributing to keep me here in this climate. But no: in spite of your forgetting me, I prefer our country and, far from affecting to conform to English manners, I enjoy displaying myself as a complete Frenchman. The English, at home, are not at all as they are abroad. But all peoples are like that. The English are much more considerate, more interested in knowing your opinion of their country, whereas I, on the contrary, feel a bit as they are when they come to France, in a mood to defend France at their expense, a thing we never do in their presence when we are at home.

Give me all kinds of news. As for the tiresome business which you have been so considerate to undertake for me, were you also kind enough to ask my caretaker to scatter some pepper in my Turkish clothes and saddles, and to have some wooden bars added to consolidate the stable for the horses? Has my nephew found lodgings?

In Wilkie's studio I saw a sketch of *Knox, the Puritan, preaching before Mary, Queen of Scots*. I cannot tell you how beautiful it is. But I'm afraid he'll ruin it; with him, it's a fatal mania.

I also saw here a play about Faust which is the most diabolical thing one can imagine. Its Mephistopheles is a masterpiece of character and intelligence. It's Goethe's *Faust*, but adapted, though the essential has been preserved. They've made an opera of it, with admixtures of comedy and also of the most gothic kind of macabre romance. The church-scene, for instance, is played with a priest singing in the distance to some organ-music. It would be difficult to be more effective in this manner, on the stage.

I also saw the *Freischütz* in two different theatres, with some music that had not been played when it was performed in Paris. There are some very odd and interesting details in the scene where they melt the lead for their ammunition. The English have a better understanding of theatrical effects than we have, and their stage-sets, which are not carried out with as detailed care as ours, are much more advantageous to the characters of the play. They have some actresses who are divinely beautiful, often worthy of more attention than the show itself. Their voices are delightful and their figures appear quite alien to this country.

Farewell, dear friend. My regards to all our friends, to Leblond and others. If you see Monsieur Rivière, whom we all love dearly, as you know, give him all my compliments and tell him that his opinions of this country seem to me quite correct. I agree fully with him: we are as good as these islanders and even better in many respects.

Please remind me too to Madame Pierret.

E.D.
13 Charles Street, Middlesex Hospital.

To M. PIERRET
London, June 27th 1825.

My dear friend,

I avail myself of M. Enfantin's return to Paris – he has been here for the past month – in order to send you some news. The longer I stay here, the more I would like to remain. The weather is fine, which is rare for London. Many friends have pitied me for not being at home for the coronation festivities, but I doubt whether my presence would have added any charm to them. I have received a letter from you and one from Edouard who continues to announce that he will soon be here. I reckon he should now be arriving any day.

The courtesy of the English towards foreigners who come to their country is extreme, and I can express but gratitude and praise for it, though the sample Frenchmen whom they have managed to obtain here are scarcely likely to give them a lofty idea of our national character. A whole crowd of people whose means of existence are somewhat dubious seeks refuge here. In London's hotels, one meets all our Paris bankrupts and forgers.

I saw *Richard the Third*, played by Kean, who is a very great actor, in spite of all that our friend Duponchel has said of him, dismissing him as England's mere 'Philippe'. I would not be able to agree. I'm not so enthusiastic about Young, whom I have seen in several plays, among them *The Tempest*, which has not been produced again. The beginning of *Richard the Third* has been changed: instead of the scene of the death of Clarence, they now have one with the death of Henry the Sixth, which is also written by Shakespeare, but originally for the second part of *Henry the Sixth*. Richard is still only Gloucester and enters the prison and kills the King with a sword. This was admirably performed by Kean, besides a thousand other details that I'll surely describe to you until you are sick of listening to my reports. I also saw Kean in *Othello*. One lacks words to express properly one's admiration for the genius of Shakespeare, who invented Othello and Iago. Tomorrow, much to my regret, I am prevented from attending a performance where Young is billed for Iago's part, with Kean playing Othello. Though each of them plays generally in a different theatre, they will now join forces on the same stage for a benefit performance. I also expect to see *Hamlet*. Mr Elmore could scarcely be more helpful to me than he is. Quite recently, I have begun to work in his establishment.

How is Felix? I hope you had enough presence of mind to give Edouard a whole batch of letters to bring to me, if only to compensate me generously for having expected him there so long. I met Mayer here; he's making a pile of money painting portraits. He regretted very much not having known that Duponchel had been in London. Mayer is, for me, the compass of fashion, as you may well believe; unfortunately, one cannot go very far in this country with modest means.

There have been several hangings since I arrived here, but I was never tempted to go and witness them. As a matter of fact, they happen each week on Monday and Friday, so that you may well imagine how convenient it is to satisfy one's curiosity in this respect, should one ever take a fancy to it – I don't remember whether I have already spoken to you of my fear of vermin that might get into the Turkish clothes and carpets that I have left in my studio.

Farewell, my good and dear friend. I embrace you tenderly and recommend myself to the kind thoughts of all who are dear to you, first and foremost to Mme Pierret.

E. Delacroix.

On the reverse side, I have written a few words for Henri. He lives, I believe, at 94 Place Beauvau.

To Monsieur PIERRET
rue de l'Université, No. 46, Paris

London, this 1st of August 1825.

My good friend,

I avail myself of a gentleman's departure to write you a few words. I have received my nephew's letter, where he writes to me about the lodgings. I suppose that is where I will have to stay or to send him anything, that is to say rue du Houssaye, No. 5. Tell him the neighbourhood and the various advantages which he mentions all delight me; but that the distance from my studio means something, and that a lease also means something. But, since things are as they are, let's no longer discuss the whole matter.

I leave London tomorrow on a little trip that will last a few days, partly on the Thames and partly at sea, aboard the yacht of one of M. Elmore's friends. I'm mad about seascapes and I'll perhaps leave shortly for Cornwall with Isabey, who is here and turns out to be a very pleasant companion. It would be a trip of some fifteen days along the wildest coasts of England, which might later be of advantage to me to compensate the expense it would cause me immediately. After that, I'll return to London, where I would no longer have much to do, so that I would soon be returning to be among all the friends who have never ceased to haunt my imagination for a single day since I left them, until I feel the distance that separates me from them all the more in this none too cheerful country. There is definitely something sad and stiff about everything here, contrasting with all that we have in France. The cleanliness of the homes and of some streets is compensated by the filth of others. The women are all sloppily dressed, with dirty stockings and badly made shoes. What strikes me most is a general atmosphere of pettiness that makes one feel that one is in a country of people whose circumstances are more straitened and tight than those we know at home. I'm even beginning to believe that people here are, if it's at all possible, more stick-in-the-mud and more addicted to old-wives' gossip.

I'm not considering all this as an economist or a mathematician. From that point of view, the English offer all sorts of advantages which I'm not willing to contest. Besides, all these impressions must naturally be, in my case, somewhat personal. I have an idea that Italy's more abandoned way of life would suit my temperament better than England's neatness. One must admit, however, that these fine green countrysides and the banks of the Thames, which are like a continuous English garden, are a delight to the eye. But it all looks like toys. It's not natural enough. I don't know by what whim of nature Shakespeare was born in this country. He is assuredly the father of their arts, but one is quite surprised to see how much method there is in their disorderly way of handling these matters.

I called on Lawrence with someone who was well enough recommended to him, so that he was very affable to us. He is a paragon of courteousness and a real painter of grandees. I'll describe him to you some day with a greater wealth of detail. In his house I saw some very fine old-master drawings and some of his own paintings, sketches and even drawings that are admirable. Never have eyes been handled, especially those of women, as well as by Lawrence, and his mouths with parted lips are perfectly charming. He is inimitable.

I cannot remember whether I wrote to you that I had seen Kean as Shylock in *The Merchant of Venice*. It's admirable and we'll discuss it together. Nothing can console me now that I have missed Young's *Hamlet*. The biggest theatres are closed and, in any case, the weather is very warm.

I've taken a fancy to riding, of all things. M. Elmore is unbelievably kind to me and acts as my riding-master. I seem to have some talents there and even went so far as to give two or three convincing performances during which I appeared to be about to break my neck. That kind of thing all helps to build one's character.

On behalf of France, I take on all kinds of Englishmen in single combat. In this people's blood, there is something quite savage and fierce that comes horribly to the surface in the rabble, which is quite ghastly. But they have an admirable government. Freedom is here no vain word. The pride of their aristocracy and the affectation of manners of other ranks are all pushed to a point that shocks me beyond words, though it has some good results.

Farewell, my great and good boy. Should I perish in the course of the tempests of my tour, I'll not die as an Englishman, but still very French indeed and your friend who is proud of this. A thousand messages to your wife and to all our friends to whom I do not write because my letters would then be all too repetitious. I cannot remember whether I wrote Felix a reply; in any case, my present letter can serve him too. I had felt a desire to return to France via Brittany and to call on his brother there, but I have an idea that it may not prove possible. For the time being, I embrace him and you too. I fear I may no longer find him in Paris if he has gone to his beloved Burgundy.

If you can still find the parcel containing the *gumwater* that Fielding sent me long ago, you would give me great pleasure by offering a good share of it to M. Auguste, who has absolutely none left at his disposal. You may all reach me at the following address:

M. Eug. Delacroix, at M. A. Elmore,

3 John Street, Edgeware Road.

I intend to bring back to Leblond a number of various curiosities that I may find, according to his instructions. In order to avoid their being unpacked and examined at Calais I'll adopt the policy of having these objects packed in a case which I'll have sealed when I land in France so as to ship it to the customs house in Paris, addressed to M. Leblond. Please inform him of this and let him tell you whether he can think of a better solution and give you the imposing title that I must add to his name as a civil servant attached to the customs-administration. I have heard of his adventures through Edouard, who was unable, however, to give me any very exact news of Mme Berger, our mutual friend who plays the part of Providence in the lives of those of us who are not blessed with legitimate spouses. You'll also let me know how Henry is faring. Ask him to remember me to my Riesener uncle and aunt. Tell Felix to do as much to all the family, to Mme Lamey and my Pastoc uncle. Give me news of Soulier, on whom I rely to transmit my respectful compliments in the rue Saint-Dominique. M. Louis Schwiter, to whom I allow myself to be *kindly* remembered, might do me the favour of letting me know through you, when you give him news of his delightful Mlle. Sophia, in which Princes Street lives the nymph for whom I have a ring. London has a good dozen streets of that name and is a vastly big city. Usually, to the name of a street, one adds that of a nearby square or of the nearest place that might distinguish it, as for instance, Charles Street, Middlesex Hospital, etc.

There should exist here some really severe courses in good taste, though one must admit that some Englishmen are quite unexceptionable. But I seem to be at odds with their women. With the exception of

Shakespeare's plays, I have seen nothing in their theatres that is not more or less clumsy imitation of what we do in France. I saw a *Barbier de Seville* and a *Mariage de Figaro* that were both precious examples of the absurd. Their music is ghastly. Even the blind here have less feeling than ours, if this is possible, for the instrumental part, whether violin, clarinette or flageolet. No matter how sentimental a tune, they'll always find a way, in their theatres, of thrusting a toot on a trumpet into it. If John Bull fails to hear, in his seventh-heaven gallery, some trumpet-work, he thinks there's no music and that the musicians have fallen asleep.

Has nothing been decided about my delightful productions which M. Laffitte appeared to want? The financial aspects of my life will very soon prove to deserve serious consideration.

To PIERRET.
London, 12th August (1825)

I have just received a letter from you, my dear friend, and am surprised that you should have had no news of me. I had written to you and I forgot to whom else, and sent these messages through a Frenchman who was returning to Paris. I presume you now have my letter, unless it's still in this gentleman's pocket. I remember that I asked you, among other things, to see whether you could find a small parcel of *gumwater* that Fielding once sent me, if you remember it, and to give it, or at least most of it, to M. Auguste, rue des Martyrs, No. 11.

Three days ago, I returned from a very pleasant trip in Essex. I went there by sea, aboard an English nobleman's yacht; he is the owner of a castle where I spent a few days. As the wind was contrary for our return trip to London, we made several excursions, in spite of some stormy weather, which allowed me to see some fairly rough seas.

On the whole, England seems to me to be rather dull. Only a very powerful motive, for instance business, might make me stay here. During all the time I have spent in this country that is glutted with gold, I have only caught glimpses of opportunities of some day working here profitably. I'll be back in Paris towards the end of the month. I found your letter yesterday when I came home in a very melancholy mood. It gave me great pleasure, Leblond's letter too. Please give him my thanks and tell him how much I appreciate your letters. You have both remained faithful to your habits and the absence of one friend never makes as noticeable difference in one's life as abandoning everything at once, though travel, when all is said and done, is a good thing in itself, providing new emotions that make us judge other countries on our own experience, then return home with pleasure.

I can see possibilities of establishing myself later in this country, though not without some apprehension. A lot of guineas would be necessary to help me digest England's monotony and make enough real friends here to let me feel time weigh less heavily on my hands. Even then, one would always regret those other real friends whom one had left at home and who were one's older friends. My best regards to Mme Pierret, Mlle Annette and M. Louis; do not forget to kiss Baptiste, Claire and Juliette on my behalf.

My dear Felix, May I expect the please of seeing you on my return to Paris? I doubt it, if you are now off to Burgundy. As usual, it will be difficult for me to become accustomed to the idea of returning to France and not finding you among the few friends whom I miss here. I now remember that you once told me you were studying English, of which I am now glad. On my return, I expect to ask you to give me a few lessons, if you have made as much headway as I expect. I'm terribly lazy and have made no attempt to practice my English here so that I have failed to make all the headway that I would have had reason to expect after some three months spent in England. Besides, as it always happens, I am now leaving this country just when I was about to begin to speak with some fluency. All the Frenchmen who are here agree that it suddenly comes to one after a few months. But I'll make up for it, I hope, when we study it together.

Most of the theatres are closed. Everyone is in the country. One no longer sees a single carriage in the streets. Those who stay in London – I mean persons of some quality – are careful not to appear in public and they hide themselves in the rooms at the back of their houses. It would be utterly indecent to be seen at all in town in this season. The only entertainment left is the English opera, but music is something that appeals to emotions which can scarecely be fostered by industry and machines. Farewell, my good friend. Remember me to your mother and all your relatives. The pleasure of seeing them again will be, for me, as great as that of embracing you.

E. Delacroix.

To MONSIEUR TH. SILVESTRE.
Paris, this 31st December 1858.

My dear Sir,

I received your letter from London and find that it is too urgent for the subject that I must now discuss and for my present condition. Quite exceptionally, for the last three days, although I had been perfectly fit for the past six months, I have now felt ill to the point of being quite prostrate. Had you asked me for this information for some later date, I might have taken my time to reply. In any case, what you ask me happens to be what gives me most pleasure to do. The memories of the period in my life when I visited England and of my few friends of those days are very pleasant to me. Nearly all these friends are no longer of this world. Of the English artists who honoured me as their guest – all of them with the greatest kindness, for I was in those years practically unknown – I think that only one is still alive. Wilkie, Lawrence, the Fielding brothers, both of them great artists, especially Copley, in landscape and water-colour, Etty too, who died recently, I believe, all of these were extremely courteous to me. I have not included Bonington in this list. He too has died in the flower of his life, but he was my personal comrade with whom – as also with Poterlet, another painter who died prematurely and in whom art lost great hopes – he was a Frenchman – I spent my time in London among all the enchantments that an enthusiastic young man can experience in that country, from a profusion of collected masterpieces and from the spectacle of an extraordinary civilization.

I no longer think of seeing London again. I would fail to find there any of these memories and especially I would no longer find myself the same man to enjoy all that can now be seen there. Even the English School has changed. I might now find myself committed to defending Reynolds and Gainsborough, that delightful artist whom you are quite right to love. Not that I am a sworn enemy of what is now being done in English painting. I have been struck too by the prodigious conscienciousness that the English can display even in matters of imagination and fantasy. It almost seems as if, returning to rendering detail with excessive care, they are more attuned to their particular genius now than when they imitated Italian painters, above all, and Flemish colourists. But is a tree's bark so important? They remain utterly English beneath this apparently new surface. Thus, instead of painting mere pastiches of the Italian primitives, as fashion now dictates here in France, they add, to their imitations of the manner of these old Schools, an admixture of infinitely personal sentiment, offering us an interest derived from the painter's own passion, an interest indeed that is generally lacking in our own cold imitations of schools and styles that have had their day.

I am writing to you as I go, without a pause, offering you all that comes to my mind. My impressions of England as I then saw it might today be corrected. I might perhaps find in Lawrence an over-exploitation of effective devices and media that reminds me too much of the school of Reynolds. But the prodigious subtlety of his draftsmanship, the life that he lends to his women who seem to speak to you, all this gives Lawrence, as a portrait-painter, his superiority over even Van Dyck, whose admirable figures pose quite calmly. The light in eyes, the parted lips of a mouth, these are rendered admirably by Lawrence.

He received me very graciously. He was indeed, above all, an extremely gracious man, except if one criticized his paintings. Two or three years after my visit to England, I sent there several paintings, among these *Greece seated on the ruins of Missolonghi* and *Marino Faliero*. The latter attracted considerable attention and I have been assured that Lawrence expressed the intention of purchasing it. But he died just about then. I once received an eight-page letter from him concerning an article I had published in the *Revue de Paris* about his portrait of the Pope. I was unwise and showed his letter, before having yet read it properly, to a passionate autograph-collector who snatched it from me and never returned it.

Wilkie was also was friendly to me as his somewhat reserved character allowed. One of my most striking memories is that of his sketch of *John Knox preaching*. Later, he made a painting of it and I have been assured that it is not as good as the original sketch. I took the liberty, when I saw it, of telling him, with typically French inpetuousness, that 'even Apollo, were he to take the brush in his own hand, could only spoil the picture by trying to finish it.' A few years later, I saw him again in Paris. He called on me to show me a few drawings which he had brought back from a trip to Spain, whence he was returning home. He seemed to have been very deeply disturbed by the paintings he had seen there. I admired him because, a man of such real genius and already almost in his old age, he could still be so deeply influenced by works so very different from his own. As a matter of fact, he died soon after that and, I have been told, in a very troubled state of mind.

Constable, an admirable man, is one of England's claims to glory. I have already mentioned him to you as well as the impression he made on me when I was painting *Le massacre de Scio*. He and Turner are true reformers. They both departed from the rut of traditional landscape painting. Our own school is now rich in talents of this kind, having learned much from their example. Géricault returned quite dazzled from seeing one of the big landscapes that Constable had sent us.

I did not happen to be in England at the same time as Charlet and Géricault. I need not tell you now what one should think of these painters. You know of my great admiration for both of them. Charlet is one of our country's greatest men; but they will never raise, here in France, a statue to a man who only played around with a little stub of a pencil to draw little figures. Poussin had to wait two hundred and fifty years for that famous public subscription for a monument to him which, I believe, has still not materialized, for lack of funds. Had he but reduced two villages to ashes, Poussin would not have had to wait long.

I pray that you will bring us here the fine works about which you write to me. Our School badly needs the experience of an infusion of new blood. It is old and the English School appears to be young. Their painters seem to be searching for more natural effects while we concern ourselves only with copying paintings. Please do not provoke my being stoned to death by attributing to me publicly these beliefs which, alas, are mine in private.

The little painting for which I regret that I made you wait so long was recently completed and I am ready to hand it to a properly accredited person if you do not prefer to wait for it until your return. You were wise to provoke me to discuss here matters of which I am fond. Now you have four whole pages from a sick man who feels somewhat refreshed by these memories. I would be very glad if all this could be of some use to you. You know my gratitude and the pleasure I experience whenever I can be of assistance to you.

Your very devoted,
Eug. Delacroix.

ON ENGLISH ART

From his *Journal,* June 17th 1855:

The next day, a Sunday, I began to think, soon after arising, about the very special charm of the English School. Its painters display a real subtlety that transcends whatever intentions merely to imitate may still crop up here and there, such as those that one can also observe in our own infelicitous School. Subtlety, with us, is the rarest of qualities: everything appears, on the contrary, to have been done with heavy tools and, even worse, by obtuse and unrefined minds. Once you have made an exception of Meissonier, Decamps and a couple of others, including the early works of Ingres, all the rest is commonplace and lacks sharpness of vision, clear intentions and warmth. One need sonly to glance through *L'Illustration,* that stupid and vulgar journal put together in France by tawdry artists, and then compare it with any similar journal published in England, and this will soon give you an idea of how cheap, nerveless and insipid most of our productions can be. Our nation claims to be the home of draftsmanship, but offers no trace of it, least of all in our more pretentious paintings. But in little sketches from England, nearly every object is handled with all the interest that it deserves: landscapes, seascapes, costumes, battle-scenes, all this is delightful, pertinently handled and, above all, *drawn*. Nowhere in France can I find anything comparable to the work of Leslie, Grant, or all those others of the English School who derive their art in part from Hogarth, but also with something of the ease and suppleness of the school of four decades ago, I mean Lawrence and his associates, whose shining virtues were their elegance and their light touch.

If one also studies another phase of their world which is quite novel, I mean what is called the 'arid' school, with its memories of the Flemish Primitives, one can still discover, beneath this surface appearance of reminiscences and in the very dryness of their technique, a real and quite local feeling for truth. How much good faith is still revealed in the midst of all this so-called imitation of older masters! Compare, for instance, the *Order for Release,* painted by Holman Hunt or Millais, I forget which, with our own French 'primitives' and 'Byzantines' whose minds are so obsessed with style and who, with their eyes always fixed on images from another age, can borrow from these only their stiffness, without ever contributing any new quality of their own. Our crowd of such sad mediocrities is huge, without a trace among them of truth, I mean of the kind of truth that comes forth from the soul. Nothing there like that child sleeping on its mother's arm, with its little head of silken hair, its sleep so full of truth and all its features, even its flushed legs and feet, depicted with a peculiarly intense power of observation and, above all, of feeling. All these painters like Delaroche, Janmot and Flandrin, that is what they call 'the grand manner'! But what can one find there, in their paintings, of the real man who painted them? How much of Giulio Romano is in the one, and then, in the other, of Perugino or even of Ingres, who was one his master?

Above all, everywhere we perceive the claims to be serious, to be a great man, and, as Delaroche says, to be producing 'serious art'.

Leys, the Flemish painter, also seems to me to be interesting, though he fails to have, in spite of his more independent manner, this utter frankness of the English artists. In his work I can detect an

element of effort, a manner, in fact something that leads me to
question the artist's absolutely good faith; and all the others of his
school fail ever to come up to him . . . Janmot has indeed seen and
studied Raphael, Perugino, etc. . . . much as the English too have
studied Van Eyck, Wilkie, Hogarth and the rest, but the English all
retain, after such studies, their own originality.

Translated by Eduard Roditi

Robert Crawford

NEC TAMEN CONSUMEBATUR

The most famous violinist on Eigg,
Denounced from the pulpit for his Gaelic folksongs,

Threw on the fire an instrument made
By a pupil of Stradivarius.

'The sooner', thundered *The Times*,
'All Welsh specialities disappear

From the face of the earth the better.'
You whose parents came from a valley

North of Hanoi are now living in Princeton
Teaching low-temperature physics. Often

When you spoke about poems in Vietnamese
I heard behind the pride in your voice

Like a *ceilidh* in an unexpected place
The burning violins of small peoples.

Hugo Williams

SUMMER NOTES

Your thoughts race ahead of you down the line
to where the day is building
a strange new town for you to arrive in,
the ruined castle,
the different-coloured buses,
the girl from the office
who tears up your day return
and throws it in pieces at your feet.

You smile for no reason
at a cut-out of two workmen
carrying a ladder across a field
on behalf of 'KARPIN BROS REMOVALS AND DECORATIONS'.
Even the horses looking up from grass
seem to agree that time and you
are flying past for once
without knowing why exactly.

*   *   *

The hotel cost too much
so we didn't even touch the bed
and said we'd decided not to take it after all
and just picked up our things
and set off down the road
till we came to this youth hostel
in an old hospital
and asked ourselves quietly
what we were doing there
and laid out the remains of the picnic
and took stock of the situation.

Get that chair over there
and we'll just sit here and talk.
It's been a long day. Our feet hurt.

Our money is running out.
When I've calmed down a bit
I'll go out and see if I can find such a thing
as a bottle of wine
in this godforsaken town.

*   *   *

When I am with you, I am a minute behind,
picking up pieces of coloured glass
and calling you back to me, 'Look . . .'

You have seen something new up ahead.
You don't look round. There you go,
scrambling over rocks on your way to the sea.

*   *   *

We leave the villa early, carrying toys,
and drift down to the beach for hangovers.
(There was sand in the bed, one of us didn't sleep.)
Every time we look up, eyes screwed against the sun,
another package screams behind the mountain,
another sailboard hits the ocean.

A vast departure lounge surrounds us with Duty Free,
Pink Floyd on the seafront p.a., time-share cowboys.
As we lie back, closing our eyes, we are fastening
our seat-belts, putting out our cigarettes, touching down.
The front door we are trying to push open
is snagged with next year's brochures.

*   *   *

The treasured routine now briefly no longer treasured
the long-distance holidaymakers drag their feet
through the stubble fields overhanging the sea.

In the fading light, they have left behind a face-mask,
whose curved breathing-tubes stick up out of the sand
like the horns of a lost war-helm.

Julia Casterton

POEM WITHOUT A SUBJECT RETURNS TO ITS START

This second daughter's loose white skin
skin not yet filled out with flesh
brings back my Nana's brown sagged neck
and wide scar where they took out the cancerous
thyroid gland. Skin once filled now void
of muscle, gristle, all the bits that beat.

And her enormous toes bring back
my double jointed mother
who could arch her back and drop down in a crab,
though we never saw her do it,
crouched in the kitchen with her fag-ends.
Black hair, dark needs, absences.
Waiting for him who didn't come, prowling for him.

Did he know about the wild animal shut up at home
while he sweated in the allotment
or dug the waste land at the side of chapel?

When she died, she left us her dark needs.
She didn't leave nothing behind. She left holes.

So my father had to fall in love again
with a woman my own age, who would not hear of it.
'Don't start that,' she said, when his tongue came loose
and made him tell her. 'When did you last see her,
Dad?' 'Last Christmas. I took her some cologne.
But we are in constant communication.
In fact, I write to her every night.'
And my foster sister had to get pregnant
at sixteen. She had holes too.
And the Heavenly Father has not intervened.
He never does, though they wait. They waited
for Rachel, dead in a car crash, to walk back through
the door. 'The Lord could uproot her from the earth
And breathe the breath of life back in' –
As if she were a Golem. Thank God I married a Jew.
And Ruth had to become an alcoholic. Filling up the holes
with vodka, till they found the bottles in her wardrobe
all done up in plastic bags. This second daughter cries.
I try to work out why. 'Even crying is a language'
the midwife said.

Paul Potts

One afternoon in November 1939 I was sitting with Tony Dickins at the bar of the Wheatsheaf in Soho. One of my companion's claims to fame was his launching of *Poetry London* in the previous year, with the Ceylonese poet Tambimuttu as editor. Dickins was in the middle of a fervent apologia for homosexuality when a youngish man with receding hair and a hungry wolfish look suddenly appeared at his elbow, greeted him brusquely and asked him if he had half-a-crown to spare, not a small sum in those days. Tony said he was unable to oblige, and began to describe the parlous state of his finances. 'All right, all right,' snapped the begging gentleman with the vulpine look. 'So you can't help me.' He moved away to seek salvation in another part of the bar. 'Who on earth was that?' I enquired. 'That,' said Tony sombrely, 'was Paul Potts. He writes poems with a socialist message and sells them as broadsheets in the streets. The poor fellow always seems to be on his uppers. He's sort of Canadian. Born over there but educated mainly in England.'

Shortly after this episode Paul, as I later learnt, joined the army as a volunteer, and I did not see him again for two or three years. Possessed of a healthy loathing of Hitler, he had been keen to make a contribution towards ridding the world of his odious presence. Paul, however, proved to be something of an embarrassment to the army for he was hopelessly maladroit and neurotically averse to any kind of discipline. In northern France – amazingly, he was serving with 12th Commando – he broke cover on a number of occasions to wander about the countryside blithely unconcerned about the proximity of the enemy and endangering his own life as well as those of his fellow soldiers.

In due course he was dispatched to London and put in charge of the regiment's canine mascot. This was hardly Paul's idea of fighting for democracy. Besides he detested dogs. He eventually managed to obtain an honourable discharge from the army.

It was about this time that I spotted him sitting alone at a table one night in the Swiss pub in Old Compton Street. (It is now a gay establishment called Compton's Bar.) The wolfish look, happily, was not in evidence. However, his hair had receded dramatically since I last saw him, but the noble dome now on display more than compensated for its loss. He had a certain presence, due partly to his clean-cut features, candid blue eyes and impressive dome. The general effect was rather let down by his food-stained clothes and dirty fingernails.

I introduced myself, found that he was disposed to be friendly and, noticing that his glass was empty, offered to buy him a drink. A Guinness was requested and duly obtained. To my surprise he downed it in about four seconds. After a while his glass seemed to be making its emptiness felt. Paul appeared not to notice, talking away about his experiences in the army. 'Another drink, Paul?' 'No, no, I don't want another drink. Yes, please. More of the same, old boy.' (As I later learnt, he had a predeliction for this upper-class term, which seemed as incongruous as if he had suddenly donned a bowler hat or produced a rolled-up umbrella.) I took his glass back to the bar to be filled again with the dark, foaming liquid, which Paul polished off as soon as it was set down. I concluded that he always drank in this extraordinary fashion. I eventually got him another Guinness, which suffered the same brutal fate as the others. Then he declared, somewhat unexpectedly, that he would like to give me a meal.

We repaired to an Italian restaurant, where we ordered spaghetti bolognese. The helpings were generous but Paul demolished his as quickly as he had his Guinness. Much of his spaghetti, however, failed to reach its intended destination and lay strewn over the tablecloth. Having smartly dispatched a black coffee, Paul announced quite casually that he was broke. So I had to foot the bill. As we were about to part company outside the restaurant Paul said: 'Can you lend me half-a-crown, old boy? Bus fares, you know, and my entrance fee to the French tomorrow morning.' I duly obliged.

Paul had apparently reverted to his pre-war state of indigence, which was relieved only by his annual grant from the Royal Literary Fund and occasional publication of a poem or an article. It was his wont most mornings to descend on Soho around pub opening time and devote the rest of the day to borrowing half-crowns and cadging meals and drinks. Those marathon tapping stints must have imposed a severe strain on his nervous system and partly accounted for his frequent outbursts of hysterical rage.

I often ran into Paul in various Soho establishments. He was usually ebullient, paranoic and talkative in a nervy sort of way but sometimes embarked on a prolonged whinge about his awful life. 'I should have been a doctor or an architect,' he would moan. 'I should have married and had children and led a civilized life. But I'm a poet, God help me. I never know where my next meal is coming from. I live in a doss house among social outcasts. Bartenders sneer at me when I enter a pub without any money for a drink. I should have been a doctor or an architect.' And so on.

The Scottish painter, Robert MacBryde, used to compare Paul to an old gramophone record. There was a period when Paul sported an American-looking trilby and, during angry denunciations of people who had humiliated him, repeatedly snatched it from his head, which was evidently in an overheated condition, and jammed it back on a minute later.

It seemed to me that having even a mundane job, teaching English to foreign students, for instance, or working in a bookshop, would have been preferable to his stressful, time-consuming method of surviving. (His lack of qualifications ruled out more remunerative and prestigious occupations.) I should have realized, of course, that his childishly hysterical temperament would have made it impossible for him to hold down a job. However, I cautiously broached the subject one day but he said that he would be worse off financially if he had a job of the kind I had in mind. This disclosure astonished me. I knew that he engaged in a spot of pilfering from time to time, but his main source of income was undoubtedly those half-crowns he so assiduously netted every day in Soho.

The victims of his light-fingered activities were mainly friends whose houses he visited – usually only once. He tended to favour silver cutlery and valuable books. On one occasion he was leaving his host at the end of a dinner party when a book slid to the floor from inside his overcoat. His host recognised it at once, since it was a collector's item that formed a part of his library. He had noticed that Paul's overcoat was bulging strangely. In icy tones he asked him to hand over the other books lurking inside his coat. Three or four were produced and grudgingly returned to their owner. Then, to the astonishment of his host, he asked him for half-a-crown. I do not know how he reacted to this impudent request but I like to think he saw the funny side and coughed up.

During the course of some Saturday night bash or other at which Paul was a guest, his host had wandered into the kitchen and found Paul leaving hastily by the garden door. Visibly startled, Paul spun round to reveal that he was wearing three of his host's best shirts. There was, too, the bizarre episode of the Radio Doctor's overcoat.

During the 'forties Charles Hill, an owlish-looking Tory MP, used to give talks on health matters on the Home Service; he thereby acquired the nickname of the Radio Doctor. He had a bluff manner that bordered on the absurd. One afternoon he dropped into the Colony Club, where he surrendered his overcoat, a posh one, to the cloakroom attendant – Bobby Hunt, an art student, who later became a book illustrator. Paul was also in the club that afternoon, having left his less posh overcoat with Bobby. When he later sought to reclaim it Bobby gave him the Radio Doctor's by mistake. It was a handsome garment which took Paul's fancy. He slipped into it, found it a good fit and made a hasty exit.

An hour or so later Bobby set out in search of Paul, clutching an old overcoat that smelled of booze and tobacco. He was feeling embarrassed and angry in equal measure. He found Paul in the French, where he was preening himself, or so it seemed to Bobby, in the Radio Doctor's expensive overcoat. Confronted by Bobby he resolutely declined to hand over the coat in exchange for his own.

But Bobby was determined not to be bested and when Paul left the pub he began to follow him at a discreet distance, weaving his way through the various streets and alley ways. Paul eventually came to a halt outside an Italian restaurant into which he disappeared. Warily peering through the window, Bobby was able to discern Paul hanging up the overcoat and sitting at an unoccupied table. Seizing this golden opportunity Bobby dashed into the restaurant, flung Paul's overcoat over a peg, grabbed the Radio Doctor's garment, made a lightning exit and jubilantly hot-footed it back to the Colony.

Paul had a tendency to let fly with deeply wounding insults for no reason at all. As a result it was not uncommon to see him sporting a black eye or swollen jaw or cuts on his face. Occasionally somebody got in first with a damaging slight but Paul could always top it.

One evening I was sitting with him in an Italian restaurant where he had just polished off a plate of spaghetti bolognese with the usual unfortunate consequences to the table cloth. He was craving a cigarette but I had none as I was non-smoker. A Sohoite we both knew was sitting at the next table and Paul asked him for a cigarette.

Bill was a lorry driver-cum-film extra. He drank heavily and had a tendency to wallop people who displeased him. At the moment he was eyeing Paul with extreme disfavour. Finally, he said: 'I don't give fags to poncy gits like you.'

'You should go back to the gutter where you belong,' snapped Paul.

Bill got to his feet and stood over Paul, beer fumes issuing menacingly from him.

'Come outside, you cunt,' he muttered thickly.

'I have no intention of coming outside,' said Paul. 'I suppose you want to hit me. Well, do it for heaven's sake and then bugger off.'

Bill looked puzzled for a moment, but duly punched Paul in the face. He raised his fist to repeat the action but thought better of it an lurched back to his table.

Within seconds a large lump had appeared on Paul's left temple but he sat there calmly as if nothing had happened and picked up the threads of our interrupted conversation. Although his head must have been aching badly he made no reference whatsoever to this ugly incident during the rest of the evening.

In later years Paul adopted the practice of delivering an insult and then adding 'Joke'. Thus: 'I don't know why I'm talking to a dreary little hack like you. Joke.' or 'You're a reactionary monster who ought to be thrown out of Christendom. Joke.' As a consequence he sustained fewer facial injuries.

In time it became clear to me that Paul suffered from a pronounced streak of madness. So I feel he was not really responsible for much of his shocking behaviour. It was as if his emotional development had been arrested in the cot. Babies, for instance, are unable to distinguish between what belongs to them and what does not, which may well explain why Paul could nick things from friends without experiencing the slightest twinge of remorse. But he was a deeply unhappy man.

It would be grossly unfair not to mention his admirable qualities, for he did have quite a few. He possessed, of course, physical courage. Indeed, he was absolutely fearless. He genuinely hated bullies, though he would sometimes accuse somebody of bullying him when the person in question was merely expressing outrage at his bad behaviour. The practice of verbally abusing and humiliating people was once prevalent in Soho, but if anybody received this sort of treatment in Paul's presence he would fly to his defence with savage invective. He invariably visited friends of his who where languishing in hospital, provided, of course, he had the fare. And he loved to give signed copies of his books to friends – I was the recipient of three. Nobody could have been less of a hack than Paul for he was incapable of penning a single sentence that did not come from the heart.

'I only want my bus fare,' Paul would say as we sat together in the French or wherever at the end of an evening. Then he would add: 'I'll take whatever you give me.' And I would discreetly slip him a bit of the ready. But if I encountered him when he was flush, a rare occurrence, he would gladly bestow on me some notes accompanied by a mock formal bow and then offer to buy me a double whisky, which I always declined in favour of half-a-bitter. I used to find his lofty mien on these occasions annoyingly condescending until I realized that he was playing the role of an honourable gentleman discharging an old debt, or something along those lines.

Since I am no authority on poetry I cannot pronounce on the merits or demerits of Paul's verse. Its begetter had no high opinion of it and eventually settled for writing prose, which, as it happens, often reads like poetry.

However, here are some examples from his one published book of verse, *Instead of a Sonnet* (1944)

Silence,
You typewriters
Adding machines keep quiet
For out of the mind of a bank clerk
A man
Is coming to birth.

and 'Instead of a Sonnet'

I have no songs of praise, no words of love
For cats or daffodils
But I have tried to leave forever in your ears
The noise that men make when they break their chains.

They have as can be seen an artless simplicity.

He only published four books altogether, three of them prose works, which can hardly be described as a substantial body of work especially as he lived to be seventy-nine. However, in view of the sort of life he led this modest output could be regarded as an impressive achievement.

Certain themes dominate his writings: the evil nature of tyranny, whether of the left or right, his romantic socialist faith, Israel (passionately pro), his extravagant hopeless love for sundry eccentric, mostly upper-class women, and his exalted vision of love itself. He also wrote about friends, some of them famous, for whom he had a high regard.

One of these was George Orwell, who is the subject of a whole chapter entitled 'Don Quixote on a Bicycle' in his autobiography *Dante Called Her Beatrice.* He captured the essence of this brave, kindly man with loving acuity. Ignazio Silone once told him that an essay on himself by Paul, which appeared in some literary magazine, was the most penetrating account of his spiritual beliefs that he had ever read. (Paul had visited him in his retreat in Switzerland, and, true to form, asked him for a loan. This Silone accorded him after a solemn rummage under his mattress.)

I much admire the last chapter in Paul's *To Keep a Sacrament,* which is about Anne Devlin, an Irish skivvy who was arrested by the British army after the 1803 uprising in Ireland and detained for four years. Throughout this period her jailors tortured, abused and humiliated her in an effort to make her reveal the whereabouts of the leaders of the rebellion with whom she had been consorting. However, in Paul's words, 'She never spoke a comma.'

Somebody once said that Paul could write marvellous sentences but was unable to manage paragraphs. This was too sweeping a judgement but there is something in it. One does feel that Paul was beginning to struggle for breath towards the end of some of his paragraphs. But he did have a way with sentences. Short and pithy, many of them qualify as aphorisms. Occasionally, however, he allowed himself to be carried away by lofty sentiments and as a result produced sentences of a gaseous, hyperbolic nature.

Paul's standards of personal hygiene were never high. He sometimes had an unwashed, unshaven look and his hands were often grubby. However, in his late sixties – by then he was sporting an unkempt, grisly beard – he acquired a body odour that can only be described as fetid. He had apparently given up taking baths and seldom washed. He suffered, moreover, from incontinence, for which he declined to seek medical treatment. He simply ignored the whole problem and as a result the most appalling accidents happened, though they appeared not to bother him in the least. As he entered a pub or room a terrible odour rapidly filled the whole place. Gaston Berlemont, the landlord of the French pub, never liked to bar anyone but he could not allow this olfactory assault on his customers to continue. He eventually decided that he would have to present Paul with an ultimatum. With this in mind he took him aside one afternoon. 'As soon as you come into the pub my customers leave in droves. You really must do something about this awful smell otherwise . . . well . . . it's quite impossible.' Paul muttered something about being bullied and shuffled out of the pub never to return. It seemed he was unwilling or unable to relinquish what had become known in Soho as the Famous Paul Potts Smell.

Having now become *persona non grata* in all his haunts Paul holed up in his Highbury flat, only venturing forth to do a spot of local shopping. A few resolutely loyal friends, most of them women, used to visit him from time to time but had to face scenes of horrifying squalor, in which excrement played an important part. Some of them

Paul Potts. A rare excursion from Soho.   *Marilyn Thorold*

even undertook the heroic task of cleaning his flat occasionally, though the fruits of their labour were shortlived.

The horror stories I heard about the squalid conditions of Paul's flat effectively discouraged me from visiting him for some years. Then one day I heard he was receiving home help on a daily basis. So I rang him up one morning to find out if it would be in order for me to drop over later, which it apparently was.

The house was early Victorian, like most of the buildings in the neighbourhood. None of the electric bells worked and the front door lacked a knocker. To make my presence known I had to resort to a vigorous demonstration of lung power. There was a muffled shout in response, a window on the first floor was opened slowly, and an ashen-faced. heavily bearded Paul peered down. 'Nice to see you, old boy,' he said. Whereupon he flung down a couple of yale keys attached to a piece of string. Both the keys and the string were encrusted with dirt.

I entered an uncomfortably warm room, where Paul was lying on a bed. A faint smell of ammonia pervaded the place but nothing worse, to my immense relief. A black and white television set by his bed flickered dimly and emitted faint sounds. (It stayed on all the time I was there.)

Clad in an old shirt Paul lay on top of the bed with his knee almost touching his chest, which gave him an oddly foetal look. I produced half a bottle of whisky from one of my pockets, having thought it imprudent to bring a whole bottle. Under its benign influence Paul began to relax and assume a more normal position on the bed.

It soon became sadly apparent that this was not the Paul I used to know. His conversation now consisted solely of verbal ejaculations separated from each other by painfully lengthy silences. The old passion and exuberance had vanished. But he was at least *compos mentis* and, thanks to his hard-working television set, well-informed on global events. He also listened with keen interest to my scraps of Soho gossip.

He was now virtually bed-ridden and depended on a Zimmer frame for slow, arduous excursions to the bathroom and kitchen. I told him I thought he must find this restrictive existence exceedingly

Paul Potts towards the end. *Photo Marilyn Thorold*

tedious but he said this was not the case at all. There were those friends of his who visited him regularly, his charming home help – she even dropped over at weekends for which, of course, she received no payment from the local council – and his ancient, much-loved television set.

His writing life, naturally, was over. Some years earlier he had talked of embarking on a new book to be entitled 'I may be White but I'm Irish'; but nothing came of it. In view of all those years of hardship and emotional torment he had endured, I could not really begrudge Paul this closing chapter of life in which, liberated from money worries by the Department of Social Security and cosseted by various charming women, he luxuriated shamelessly in abandoned indolence.

He was touchingly anxious to be a good host but had no food or drink in the flat. To remedy the situation he asked me to do a spot of shopping for him. On the floor beside the bed stood a large, open tin with coins of various denominations topped by a thick layer of bank notes. (This was ironic in view of all those decades of penury.) He extracted a couple of tenners and gave them to me. I made a list of the things he wanted and set out for the shops.

I returned half-an-hour later laden with various goodies. Having eaten recently I settled for a few grapes. But Paul, lying flat on his back, set about demolishing a bag of peanuts, several bananas, a bunch of grapes, a large slab of nut chocolate and a vanilla ice-cream cone. Before long his beard had acquired splodges of ice-cream, which he made no attempt to wipe away. He occasionally grabbed a mug from his bedside table and took a noisy gulp of lager laced with whisky. From time to time he emitted a loud, prolonged belch.

In the middle of the fray Susan, his home help, let herself into the flat. Youngish and attractive, she somehow suggested a ballet mistress. 'Paul,' she exclaimed, 'you know you mustn't eat lying on your back.' Paul merely grunted and continued noisily to scoff. Susan now issued a command. 'Paul, be sensible and sit up.' 'Oh, do stop bullying me,' cried Paul. But Susan kept on insisting that he obey her. Suddenly he erupted into a steam of hysterical abuse in which four-letter words played a prominent role. Susan, however, stood her ground and eventually he calmed down and then, looking exceedingly cross, heaved himself up to a sitting position.

Susan told me later that Paul's practice of guzzling food in a supine position when she was not there had landed him in hospital a few weeks earlier. Lumps of unmasticated food had accumulated in the lower part of his oesophagus and had had to be removed by means of a pump. Much of this detritus proved to be in a rotting condition.

I always turn with dread every morning to the obituary page of *The Times*. One morning I found myself confronted on this page by a photograph of Paul. It was taken when he was old and bearded.

His death had been dramatic. Alone in the flat one evening he had been smoking his pipe and accidentally set light to his bed. Neighbours, alarmed by the smoke pouring out of his flat, telephoned for the fire brigade. When the firemen burst into his room he was alive but badly burned, so badly in fact that much of his central nervous system had been destroyed. This meant he was at least experiencing no pain. He indignantly ordered the firemen to leave, an injunction, of course, they did not take seriously. Ambulance men duly arrived. However, Paul, unaware of the serious nature of his injuries, protested vigorously when they transferred him from his bed to a stretcher. They rushed him off to hospital where he died within a few hours.

Contributors

PAUL LAMBAH grew up in the Black Country and was educated at Epsom, Cambridge and the Westminster Hospital. PARINA STIAKAKI was born in Boston in 1949, but grew up in London, where she attended the London School of Economics. She lives in Crete, and her stories have been published in both Greek and English. STEPHEN FOTHERGILL was born in East London. He was a conscientious objector during the war, working on the land and as a fire-watcher in Fleet Street. Since then his jobs have included teaching, lamp-lighting, book-running and operating the lighting in West End theatres. LUCIEN STRYK lives in Illinois. He has written several books of poems, and is the editor of *The Penguin Book of Zen Poetry*. BILLIE LYDIA PORTER has worked in publishing for several years; her only previous work to be published is an article on geriatric cats and dogs. She lives in Maryland. GREGORY STRONG took his undergraduate degree in the Creative Writing Department of the University of British Columbia. He is currently working in China on an aid project for the Canadian International Development Agency. CHARLES DRAZIN was born in 1960 and educated at Oxford. He is an editor with Hamish Hamilton.

My Sporting Life

Vardens Road was in the news recently. The wife of a young couple who lived there was stabbed to death, more than fifty wounds being inflicted by the husband's mistress with the complicity of her sister. The name stirred memories. Vardens Road is at the point where Battersea becomes Wandsworth, and is not much more than a hundred yards long. It runs between two main roads, St John's Hill to one side and the Wandsworth Common end of Battersea Rise on the other. There are Victorian houses, a few pleasant the rest ordinary – in one of them the murder took place – and the road is now quite busy, a cut between the two main roads. When I was young it was dark and dozy, and contained the hall where I played table tennis. Or the place where I ended up playing, for my club Clapham had no proper home.

We graduated to Vardens Road from cramped conditions at Clapham Junction YMCA about which opponents complained, followed by an upstairs room at the Craven pub in Lavender Hill which we were asked to leave because our few members (never more than a dozen) did too little drinking. The Vardens Road hall, a billiards hall with three or four table tennis tables we hired for match and practice evenings, was more tolerant. We stayed there until I gave up table tennis in disgust at loss of form, and my brother Maurice joined another club and then became a coach. With our departure Clapham Table Tennis Club ceased to exist.

Vardens Road reminded me of how much my first quarter-century was devoted to competitive sport and games. The bits about this in some autobiographical sketches, *Notes From Another Country,* don't quite convey the major part games played in my life then. I look back on it with astonishment. How can I have wasted eleven years working in the office of a small engineering company, the only alleviations of boredom writing poems, running a little verse magazine in the last three of those years, and playing cricket, snooker and table tennis? I can't find any answer that's at all congenial, except that old inadequate excuse about the difficulty of getting a job in the Thirties. Yet my sporting life in that time does have its interest, as something typical of a period and a way of life among what in those years I learned to call the petty bourgeoisie.

In fact my sporting life began with boxing. The excellent Battersea state school called Wix's Lane that provided my education had a headmaster, new in my time, who was tremendously keen on manly sports and physical education. Gym periods were extended, so that we played a good deal of handball, did various exercises, and were encouraged to jump over a vaulting horse – something I never managed, either at school or later in the Army. On Friday afternoons the last two periods were replaced by boxing. A ring was rigged up in the main hall, and small and larger boys threw mostly harmless punches.

The school possessed, however, a boy named George Kirby who was England champion at his age (the school leaving age was fourteen) and weight. Not surprisingly, nobody wanted to go into the ring with him even for a couple of rounds. George and I were friendly, and on the understanding that he would pull his punches I agreed to be his sparring partner. It wouldn't be too much to say that our meetings became the star turn of the Friday sessions. There was no winner in these contests, and I am sure George did pull his punches. I did, however, land occasional blows, and he replied in more powerful kind. We wore no helmets or gum shields, and the result was that George knocked bits off my two top front teeth, damaging the nerves. They were crowned, in due course the crowns became loose, and had to be replaced by a small plate. Encouraged by these weekly bouts with George I entered for a London Boys' Boxing Championship, and felt myself to be the real McCoy when I had an adult second who wiped my face and murmured phrases between our three rounds, of which I can remember only: 'Get nearer to him, you've got to get inside him'. I lasted the three rounds, lost, and gave up boxing which I'd never much liked.

I had a desire to excel: my life at that time would have found complete fulfilment if I had been a good cricketer. That, alas, was never the case. I was probably a worse cricketer than I had been a boxer. Our school team won the local league thanks in part to a master who spent a good many evenings coaching us on Clapham Common (as I said, it was an excellent school), and I played for the team without distinction. Later an old boys' team was founded, which we called the Old Wixonians. Like Clapham Table Tennis Club later on we were handicapped by lack of money, and of course by lack of a home ground. For home matches we had to hire public pitches at Motspur Park and Raynes Park. Some of the teams who played us on these pitches were disgusted, and cancelled the fixture in the following season, but we had three or four unusually good players at this level of club cricket, and were eventually able to become a wandering side. I have written elsewhere about Bonzo, our leg-spinner, but there were also some useful batsmen including little Charlie Darling who eventually married a camp-following girl I briefly fancied myself in love with, a non-Wixonian Australian named Owen Barclay who somehow got into the team, and the wicket-keeper Douglas Dawson. In this odd collection the intellectual level was not negligible. Douglas was an admirer of Wyndham Lewis and elaborated ingenious theories about the relationship between food and sex, an aspiring musician friend of mine played occasionally (he became a school teacher), and Charlie's printing firm produced an issue of my magazine *Twentieth Century Verse,* although I parted company from them when they insisted on the change in one of Roy Fuller's poems from 'Lord Ashby' to 'Lord Zarley', for fear of libel. 'I suppose better Zarley than a libel action up our arses', Roy wrote to me, but that was the only issue handled by Sussex Printers.

What was my role in this useful team? I had no right to a place in it on merit, for on that level I was a sort of Major Lupton, who became Yorkshire's captain in the Twenties when an amateur was still thought indispensable in that role. Major Lupton batted number eleven, and was said to do what he was told by old stagers like Wilfred Rhodes and Emmot Robinson in the way of field placings and bowling changes. In the matter of theory, though, I was no Major Lupton – a blend of Napoleon and Wellington rather, or perhaps a Garnet Wolseley, that brilliant strategist in the end undone by his own deviousness. I was responsible for the choice of our cap and blazer colours, a tasteful purple, black and white, and the others listened dazzled (well, most of them were dazzled) as I told them just how fields should be set for each of our bowlers, the way in which they could be changed most easily for left-handers, and so on. What could they do but make me captain? And a reasonably successful captain I remained until the club disintegrated after a few years as such make-shift groupings do, some moving out of London, others losing interest, few newcomers joining. I batted low down in the order, but rarely at number eleven – a captain, after all, must have some privileges. In one match I even opened when our usual openers were having a bad run, and managed to survive until forty runs were on the board. My feeling of having done a good job was severely damaged when my fellow-opener said afterwards that this shouldn't happen again. 'Frankly, it makes the team look bad, having someone like you opening.'

Cricket was my summer game, snooker and table tennis occupied autumn and winter evenings. I have said something eleswhere about the Temperance Billiards Halls where I played, without stressing sufficiently their unusual nature. The buildings dotted about London, and especially South London, were similar in style, externally resembling squat temples with a small central dome. Within, worshippers were crouched over green baize. The Lavender Hill hall where I mostly played was probably the toughest in South London and there were only a couple of elderly attendents, yet I never saw any attempt made to bring in drink, by glass, bottle or flask. In my several years of playing there perhaps half-a-dozen fights took place, in a couple of which knives were drawn, but as far as I remember nobody was seriously hurt or arrested. The general atmosphere can only be called reverent.

It is impossible to imagine the ban on alcohol being observed in these days of canned beer, or to believe that the same comparative hush would obtain. Noise is an invariable companion of games today, and if the Temperance Halls still existed (the last one was converted long since to office, factory or, in the case of Lavender Hill, shops), they would no longer be sacerdotal but loud with the sound of radios, or simply of shouting human voices. It is true that the air was then blue with the smoke caught in the light of the lamps over the tables, and I suppose would be cleaner today.

One mark of being a serious rather than a casual player was to have your own cue, which was hung in one of the metal cases round the hall. The purchase of a cue for £2, half my weekly pay at the time, marked my awareness of entry into the Hall's elite, those likely to be considered for the Lavender Hill team. There were eight players in the team, matches were played weekly against other halls, and to play on your home tables and in front of your home crowd was as big an advantage as in soccer. Team selection was taken seriously by Tom Torr, the building worker who was our captain. I made the team at number eight two or three times but lost, in part I think through nerves, and was not chosen again.

What was the level of play, and how good a player was I? The best player I saw then, in my own Hall or elsewhere, was a gambler called Jack the Fiddler who played only for money, and had no interest in the team. I saw Jack make several seventies and eighties but never a century break, and did not myself top forty-odd. By present-day standards that may seem absurdly poor, and the fact is that the sophistication and subtlety very young players show now because they have watched the masters on TV was simply not available then. Very likely there were boys in the Thirties with the inherent potting genius of Jimmy White, but they couldn't have made a living from the game, and so had no inducement to develop their talent. Even Jack the Fiddler, who offered other players one to four blacks and played them for a fiver, regarded snooker as no more than a sideline, his real occupation being that of a fence for jewellery.

By the standard of the time, then, I was fairly good, stronger as a safety player than a potter. If I had been able to watch Steve Davis playing those marvellously precise shots that show a perfect understanding of the angles of the table and speed of the cloth, I don't doubt that I should have been much better. When I lived at Streatham during the early part of World War II I used to play Roy Fuller at the Streatham Hall, and gave him several blacks to make an even game of it. When Roy learned of the wartime arm operation that left me with a stiff, fixed left wrist he wrote: 'Will you be able to make a bridge for your cue? That seems to be important'. And the operation did spell the end of me as a snooker player. Making a bridge was at first awkward, then difficult, finally impossible, so that the only time I could play a shot steadily was when using a rest. In my prime should I have beaten those literary snooker players Martin Amis and Julian Barnes? The belief that I should must be an act of faith.

And so, briefly, to table tennis, the only game at which I was for a couple of seasons very good, though never quite England class. I've written about this in *Notes*, and have little to elaborate on here, although I think I exaggerated the speed of my decline. I certainly remained a reasonable good league player for a couple of years after my one very successful season. I was probably like many county batsmen who look very good until bowlers cotton on to some weakness like a tendency to fence at rising balls outside the off stump, and an inability to conquer it brings them down. In my case it was a backhand on which I was able to defend efficiently enough, but never able to attack with a powerful topspin drive. (Compare Steffi Graf, in that respect only.) Hence the word went round that if you concentrated on my backhand . . .

This kind of sporting life is one that no longer exists. Today a club like the Old Wixonians would be playing in a league with a limited number of overs allotted to each side, snooker at all levels is keener and sharper, and the great table tennis players of my day, Barna and Bellak and Bergman, would be lost for pace against the dancing demons of Japan and China, or our own Desmond Douglas. In the new world where in all active sports athleticism is supreme much has been lost as well as gained. The grace of Gower would always be a rarity, but there were some county batsmen in my youth whose casual elegance would be frowned on today, and the effortless ease of Viktor Barna's play could have no place in the table tennis world where power and speed are the factors that count. Yet to compare Barna and the latest dancing demon, Rod Laver with Bill Tilden, Gooch or Botham with Jack Hobbs, is not to compare like with like. The instruments of the games, and hence their techniques, have changed so much that no comparison is possible.

What prompted that eagerness to succeed in some sport or game? The easy, and I daresay right, answer is an attempted compensation for some inadequacies of childhood. Enjoyment came into it too, but there was something beyond enjoyment, and I can no more explain it than I can my immersion in Victorian military history for a few years at the end of the Fifties, and the writing of two books about it. With the books written interest died, was as though it had never been. I look back on my sporting life with similar wonder and incomprehension. It belongs in every sense to a lost world.

Gavin Ewart

MADAME LABORDE SPEAKS

'But upon the whole, in the course of my trade there have been but three escaped without doing business. Two of them had turned their brains with reading *Pamela* and *The Whole Duty of Woman,* and the last was so formed by nature that she was never intended to be made a woman of. But I have taken care to remove all such bad books out of their way and, in the stead, I generally leave *The Memoirs of a Woman of Pleasure* with cuts, or such lascivious prints for those who cannot read, as may tend to inflame their passions.' – John Cleland, *The Memoirs of Maria Brown* (1766)

No, it isn't like Tennyson's *Maud*.
It's a very hard life being a bawd,
when the girls won't use talents
for fleecing the gallants,
to delay and deceive and defraud.

Though it's terribly often the clergy
who get horny and hot-frocked and urgey –
and a good girl will pardon
a bishoply hard-on
when the blessèd champagne is all splurgey,

and I don't in the slightest or least
blame the jimp jesuitical priest –
their hats go to their heads
and they jump into beds
like a halfback (or half two-backed beast).

And it's often an English Milord
who is strolling around feeling bored –
just by closing one eye
they can make him come by
and ejaculate what he has stored.

When they once get a bird and a bottle
they will shoot off in joy, at full throttle;
though they're young ones indeed
they will learn at full speed –
though what they learn's not Aristotle.

Oh, yes. They are happy to spend
in the company of a good friend.
A girl earns a new sack
on the flat of her back –
and this will be, world without end.

I steer clear of the military men –
they will pay only if, but and when –
they will strut by like cocks
and they want girls in flocks
but they won't pay the price of one hen.

So I know that I'm part of the Plan
(while the ginger is hot, by Saint Anne,
it's all done by fine looks
and by reading good books)
that the God of the French has for Man.

A. D. HARVEY

The Nipple in Art

Examination of the pages of *Playboy* or *Mayfair* (or of one's own chest in a mirror) reveals that the human nipple is surrounded by an area, perhaps an inch in diameter, of slightly darker pigmentation, which is called the areole. Examination of nude paintings in any gallery reveals that, prior to about 1830, European artists almost never seem to have taken account of this phenomenon.

Occasionally the nipple was depicted as a minute pink blob. Where the subject of the painting required the nipple's projecting quality to be emphasized, as in Bronzino's 'Venus, Cupid, Folly and Time' in the National Gallery, where Cupid lightly squeezes Venus's left nipple between two fingers, or in Sebastiano del Piombo's 'Martyrdom of St Agatha' in the Pitti, Florence, where St Agatha's nipples are being torn off with pincers, the artist showed the nipple as protruding but almost colourless: but generally the female breast was depicted simply as a round white, nippleless, featureless swelling.

Even the plates in Govard Bidloo's *Anatomia humani corporis* (Amsterdam 1685) show the nipple as unpigmented, except in one drawing of a dissected breast. Bidloo's work was the standard treatise on anatomy for nearly a hundred years: William Cowper's *The Anatomy of Humane Bodies* (Oxford 1698), which was the authoritative text in eighteenth-century Britain, was little more than a bare-faced piracy of Bidoo's book.

Ironically, the one case where painters were disposed to show the human areole was in the depiction of the male body: expecially that of Christ on the Cross. This was because the traditional iconography of Christ emphasized his mortal, fleshly status: the New Testament story, as interpreted by the Catholic Church, was meaningless without the recognition that, in taking on human form, God had taken on fleshly corruption and fleshly weaknesses.

Occasionally, in German drawings of witches, or paintings of the damned suffering the torments of Hell, pigmented nipples are shown but this is because, as with Christ on the cross, the emphasis is on the corruptibility of the flesh.

Artists of the sixteenth and seventeenth centuries were disposed to edit out the human nipple because they believed in presenting ideal images of beauty. The influence of classical sculpture was important here. It seems probable that the sculptures of the classic Athenian period were painted in glorious technicolor, but two thousand years of exposure to sun and rain, or burial in the earth, had removed all traces of colouring. When artists began to study ancient sculpture in the Renaissance, one of the first lessons they learnt was that ideal beauty in the human body did not include pigmentation or body hair.

It was not that men had no interest in women's breasts. The Puritan Thomas Hall published a tract entitled *The Loathsomeness of Long Haire . . . With an Appendix against Painting Spots, Naked Breasts, &c* in 1653 and in 1678 a work by the French divine Boileau appeared in a London edition as *A Just and Seasonable Reprehension of Naked Breasts and Shoulders:* it claimed that women 'know as well as men, that the beauty of the bosome hath this property, that it almost continually inspires dishonest sentiments.'

In the eighteenth century Richardson's Pamela was indignant when Squire B. 'put his hand in my bosom' and in Richardson's next novel, *Clarissa,* Lovelace tells us how 'with my other hand, [I] drew aside the handkerchief that concealed the beauty of beauties, and pressed with my burning lips the charmingest breast that ever my ravished eyes beheld.' In 1745 an author using the pseudonym Lemuel Gulliver wrote a teatise entitled *Pleasures and Felicity of Marriage* of the typical wedding night when 'Those panting, snow-white Breasts, which before you hardly could presume to look upon, much less touch with one Finger, you may survey all over with eager Eyes, and imprint with burning Kisses'. Meanwhile poor Dr Johnson had to confess that he dared not venture behind the scenes at the theatre because 'the silk stockings and white bosoms of your actresses excite my amorous propensities.'

Londa Schiebinger has argued that from the mid-eighteenth century the medical profession began to recognize the need for a more accurate depiction of sexual organs, in anatomical literature at least. J.

Gautier d'Agoty Senior's *Anatomie des Parts de la Génération de l'Homme e de la Femme* of 1773, one of the first anatomical treatises to have colour illustrations, may well have been the first publication to show a woman with sepia-coloured nipples, though Bidloo's chastely monochrome breasts were served up yet again in Andrew Bell's *Anatomia Britannica: a System of Anatomy* as late as 1798.

Three years after Gautier d'Agoty published his colourful prints, incidentally, the sculptor Houdon got into trouble at the Paris Salon with his life-size 'Diane Chassereuse'. This plaster model showed neither nipple nor pubic hair, but the authorities objected to Houdon's attempt to indicate the vulva. The plaster model was barred from the Salon, and in the marble and two bronze versions Houdon later produced of his work, there was no indication of any female sexual organs at all.

As the example of Houdon shows, even artists who wished to attempt a new fidelity to nature did not necessarily depict all that was before their eyes. In the early nineteenth century the leading painter of the female nude in Britain was William Etty. By the 1830s he was regularly making pointy, pigment-ringed nipples a feature of his voluptuous nudes: he was the first commercially successful painter in Britain, perhaps in the whole of Europe, to do so. But one is struck by the peculiarly compacted anatomy of his women's bodies, which appear to belong to one of Picasso's earlier periods. Small high breasts had been regarded as normative in Western art since the fifteenth century, but even the School of Fontainebleau had never shown bosoms sprouting from collar bones as frequently as in the paintings of Etty.

Etty was something of a pioneer. Even Delacroix's 'Liberty at the Barricades' exhibits no more than a vague rosiness at the tips of her breasts: the distinct areoles shown on the version used on the modern French one-hundred franc note have been supplied by the Banque de France. Nevertheless nipples were standard in French nude painting by the 1860s, though in Britain despite – or because of – the example of Etty, artists like Burne-Jones and Alma-Tadema continued to restrict themselves to a discretely tinted dot on each bulge.

The nipple also crept slowly into literature. In 1840, in his treatise

Bronzino. Allegory of Venus and Cupid.

On the Anatomy of the Breast, Sir Astley Cooper wrote, 'The breasts, from their prominence, their roundness, the white colour of their skin and the red colour of the nipples, by which they are surmounted, add great beauty to the female form' and Edwin Arnold, editor of the *Daily Telegraph*, wrote of 'the rosy breast-blossoms/Love's rubies' in his best-selling epic about Gautama Buddha, *The Light of Asia,* in 1879.

At first glance the obvious reason for artists' rediscovery of the areole is the development of photography, which, one might have thought, ended the artist's conscious control over which details appeared in his pictures. In fact many of the earliest photographic studies of nudes have been retouched: interestingly enough the tendency was to touch out the pubic hair and to touch in the nipples, which often lacked adequate definition in pictures taken with the primitive cameras of the mid-nineteenth century. Incidentally, many nude studies were ostensibly produced for the use of painters: Delacroix produced a small odalisque based on a photo in 1857: the photo has survived and shows large, darkly pigmented areoles, which do not appear in the painting.

The work of Etty (who died in 1849), and early photos where the nipple has to be touched in, suggests that photography was not the prime reason for the rediscovery of the nipple. In the past, the most various developments have been attributed to the influence of the Industrial Revolution: here is another. The increased use of machinery was accompanied by a considerable degree of popular interest in the new technology and, it was claimed in 1811 by the author of *An Essay on Mechanical Drawing,* 'an increased demand for the journals of science and the records of those improvements'. Industry in general, and the publishing industry in particular, consequently found an increasing need for people who could make technical drawings. At the same time, a new technique for reproducing drawings, lithography, so reduced the price of reproducing pictures of whatever complexity that the total market for illustrative material, technical as well as non-technical, expanded extremely rapidly, particularly in the 1820s and 1830s. More and more work meant more and more artists – Pigot and Co's *London & Provincial New Commercial Directory* for 1828-9 lists over 580 in London alone – and more and more drawing masters

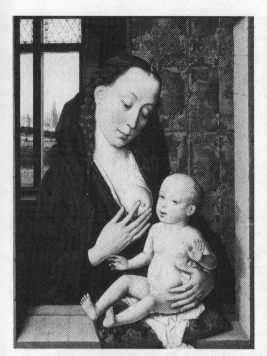

Dieric Bouts, Virgin and Child.   L. Cranach, Cupid complaining to Venus.

setting up business to teach other people to draw.

Since the early Renaissance most painters had been carefully schooled within a kind of apprenticeship system. The various established conventions of painting and sculpture had been handed down from generation to generation, and since most artists expected (and needed) to earn a living wage from the exercise of their art, experimentation was not particularly encouraged. Later, when state-sponsored academies were established, it became ever riskier than before to defy prevailing aesthetic conventions. In the later eighteenth century various challenges developed to the authority claimed by the academics, but the sudden very rapid expansion of the art profession, so to speak below and to one side of the established system of artistic apprenticeship, came close to blowing away the artistic conventions altogether. A young man might be trained to draw so that he could draw steam engines, but once he had gained confidence in his pencil there was nothing to prevent him drawing anything else.

In the sixteenth century the invention of printing had rapidly dissolved the clergy's near monopoly of book-learning. Similarly, in the early nineteenth century, new technical means of reproducing illustrations – and new types of demand for illustrations – seems to have dissolved the near monopoly of conventionally trained artists over artistic representation. After that Page Three of the *Sun* was only a matter of time.

William Etty, Nude.

The Zen Poetry
of Death

In all literature can there be poetry so all-encompassing as the Zen poetry of death, with its history of nearly 1,500 years? In T'ang China of the sixth century the first Ch'an (Zen) masters, accepting responsibilities that went with guiding a new generation, understood the exemplary nature of their role. Disciples were to be rescued from illusion, from dualistic traps set around them in a rigidly structured, Confucian, conditioned society. Only tough disciplines of Zen could possibly achieve that. The masters lived in every sense alongside their disciples, meditating and chanting with them, eating and sleeping with them, and of course making them talk out their fears, weaknesses, and hopes. They gave them koans to grapple with, again and again expressing dissatisfaction with their efforts, driving them ever harder to see, to surpass themselves.

In early days of Zen the vision of enlightenment and what it might achieve was very pure. All stages of progress in discipline were gauged scrupulously, every hour offering its special challenge. How that challenge was met was carefully judged, whether working in the vegetable garden, washing dishes, raking leaves, relating to fellows in the zendo, the daily begging round among laymen. All such things were done by the master himself, done well in order for him to receive *inka* (testimonial to the disciple's enlightenment) from his own master. He would not only have had to perform such normal functions well, in the proper spirit, demonstrating growth in discipline, but – far more important – would have had to experience in the judgment of his master, satori.

Zen's awareness of the spiritual potential of art, all arts, came early. It was especially there that its connection with China's indigenous Taoism was apparent. Perhaps more than any spiritual discipline before or since, it would maintain that it was possible to realize oneself through the practice of a *do* (Tao, or Way): *Gado* (painting),

Shodo (calligraphy), *Kado* (poetry), etc. Its masters, often expert in one or more of the arts, expected disciples to show strong interest in one or the other from the earliest period of training.

The art most accessible to Zen communities, one of its richest depositories of wisdom, was poetry, which even in early China had an ancient tradition, as in the Confucian *Book of Songs*. In order to do well in the annual state examinations, of crucial importance to all seeking advancement in the world, an appreciation of poetry was essential. Thus it was natural that disciples of a gifted master, who often employed poetry in his *teisho* (brief lectures to the assembled monks), might write *agyo* (poems of koan interpretation) such as the following by Seigensai of the twelfth century:

This grasped, all's dust –
The sermon for today.
Lands, seas. Awakened,
You walk the earth alone.

Seigensai had satori when he solved the koan 'Maitreya preaches this', and his master approved the poem as evidence of the disciple's awakening. But very few agyo were approved, thus the disciple was forced to try again and again, sometimes choosing to interpret in normal speech. After twenty years of serious application he was certain, on rolling up the blind in his room, that he had gained satori:

Rolling the bamboo blind, I
Look out at the world – what change!
Should someone ask what I've discovered,
I'll smash this whisk against his mouth.

When the poem was rejected as inadequate, he wrote the following, which more than satisfied his master:

All's harmony, yet everything is separate.
Once confirmed, mastery is yours.
Long I hovered on the Middle Way,
Today the very ice shoots flame.

There was one type of Zen poems, *jisei* (death poem), which was in a sense reserved for the master. Such a poem, sometimes composed well before death was thought to be the expression of his very being. Jisei were thus considered of great importance, not only as personal testimonial, but as virtual koans themselves. They were pondered, lectured upon, and held to be revelatory of the deepest truths of discipline. Six hundred years after the first were composed in China, they were to take their honoured place in Japanese Zen practice.

One of the most remarkable features of death poems, wherever written, is their stoicism, which when one considers the Buddhist attitude to death is not surprising. From the time of the Buddha himself it was considered essential to accept impermanence, without futile attempts to escape it. In the famous story of Kisagotami we find the Buddha dealing with an extreme case of delusion. After Kisagotami's son died she simply refused to accept the fact, carrying his dead body everywhere. A wise man of her village told her to go to the Buddha, who assured her that there was a medicine which could cure her son, but in order to prepare it he would have to have a handful of mustard seeds gathered at households which had never been visited by death. Kisagotami returned to the Buddha not only empty-handed but stripped of her delusion. Burying her son, she got on with her life. Here are two anecdotes much admired in Zen communities of Japan:

Dokuon was very sick, and Tekisui came to ask after him. Entering the sickroom, he announced himself, then straddled Dokuon. With his face almost touching Dokuon's, he said, 'Well, how are you?' 'Sick,' answered Dokuon. 'Think you'll pull through?' 'No.' Without another word, Tekisui got up and left.

A few days before Tekisui's own death, Keichu came from afar to ask about him. 'I hear,' he said to the porter, 'the master's very sick.' 'Yes, sir,' said the porter. 'Here's a box of cakes for him. When you hand it to him, give him this message: "You're old enough to die without regret."' With that Keichu left. When the porter brought the cakes to Tekisui and gave him Keichu's message, the master smiled sweetly, as if he had forgotten all pain.

When a rebel army took over a Korean town, all fled the temple except the Abbot. The rebel general burst into the temple, and was incensed to find that the master refused to greet him, let alone receive him as conqueror. It was as if he feared nothing. 'Don't you know,' shouted the general, 'that you are looking at one who can run you through without batting an eye?' 'And you,' said the Abbot, 'are looking at one who can be run through without batting an eye!' The general's scowl turned into a smile. He bowed low and left the temple.

Conditioned by training to accept life's inevitability, and feeling they might inspire disciples by demonstrating strength and serenity,

Zen masters wrote their death poems and made them public. Here is the great master Daito's poem:

To slice through Buddhas, Patriarchs,
I grip my polished sword.
One glance at my mastery,
The void bites its tusks!

But before achieving the right to be heard at such a moment, Daito had to prove himself worthy of being followed by a generation of disciples exerting great effort to raise themselves before him. They listened to his subtle lectures and had confrontations with him during *dokusan* (meeting of master and disciple for discussion of koans and related matters). All knew, had examined carefully, his satori poem, which had convinced Daito's own master that he had won through:

At last I've broken Unmon's barrier!
There's exit everywhere – east, west; north, south.
In at morning, out at evening; neither host nor guest.
My every step stirs up a little breeze.

The relationship between master and disciple is often very lengthy, sometimes more intimate than that between the disciple and his parents. The master's death may overwhelm the disciple, but at the same time steel him for the traumas of his own life, especially at the end. One can easily imagine the effect of Fumon's death poem on disciples:

Magnificent! Magnificent!
No-one knows the final word.
The ocean bed's aflame,
Out of the void leap wooden lambs.

The astonishment of Kukoku's:

Riding backwards this wooden horse,
I'm about to gallop through the void.
Would you seek to trace me?
Ha! Try catching the tempest in a net.

And Zekkai's:

The void has collapsed upon the earth,
Stars, burning, shoot across Iron Mountain.
Turning a somersault, I brush past.

How different from these wild challenges to the void is this, by
Bokuo, with its reference to the ox, an animal closely connected with
Zen, the taming of which is symbolic of enlightenment:

For seventy-two years
I've kept the ox well under.
Today, the plum in bloom again,
I let him wander in the snow.

The poem's serenity is palpable, as is this much more literal poem by
Baiho, titled 'On Entering His Coffin':

Never giving thought to fame,
One troublesome span of life behind,
Cross-legged in the coffin,
I'm about to slough the flesh.

The Chinese masters were on the whole more explicit in their *jisei*,
even giving their ages, as in Fuyo-Dokai's:

Seventy-six: done
With this life —
I've not sought heaven,
Don't fear hell.
I'll lay these bones
Beyond the Triple World,
Unenthralled, unperturbed.

The Triple World, in Zen, is that of desire, form and spirit. Here is
another such piece, by Unpo Bun-Etsu;

Sixty-five years,
Fifty-seven a monk.
Disciples, why ask
Where I'm going,
Nostrils to earth?

Just as the master is constantly challenging his disciples, the boldest are as likely to challenge him. Thus the last three lines of the poem. A number of Zen anecdotes concern confrontations in which the disciple bests his master:

Pointing to the sea, Master Kangan said to his disciple Daichi: 'You speak of mind over matter – well, let's see you stop those boats from sailing.' Without a word the young disciple pulled the *shoji* (screen) across their view. 'Hah,' the master smiled and placed the *shoji* in position again. 'But you had to use your hands.' Still without a word, Daichi then closed his eyes.

Small wonder Daichi was himself to become a great master, whose death poem inspired countless monks well beyond his own time and place:

Thoughts arise endlessly,
There's a span to every life.
One hundred years, thirty-six thousand days:
The spring through, the butterfly dreams.

From the moment the Zen master enters his zendo he is committed to a life of guidance, entering into lasting and deeply caring bonds with his disciples. In many of the death poems, as we have seen, he seems to be speaking well beyond the grave, addressing not only followers, but all men. The tenth-century Chinese master Hofuku Seikatsu, waiting to die in the mountains, made this farewell poem standing on a bridge spanning the Dokei Gorge:

Don't tell me how difficult the Way.
The bird's path, winding far, is right
Before you. Water of the Dokei Gorge,
You return to the ocean, I to the mountain.

We can assume from this that disciples often complained to him of the obstacles placed before them, and the poem was meant to further encourage them to seek the Way in nature itself. An even more remarkable instance of truth revealed by nature is found in the eighth-century Chinese master Daibai's poem, which he recited while sitting in meditation with his followers, saying aloud for their instruction, 'No suppressing arrival, no following departure':

I'm at one with his, *this* only.
You, my disciple,
Uphold it firmly –
Now I can breathe my last.

What is the 'this' referred to? A weasel's shriek, simply that. It is said that on reciting the poem he died.

It is clear that without the anecdote about Daibai's last hour his death poem would be meaningless. When one knows that he was moved spontaneously by a weasel's shriek, as if summoned by death, then the poem is seen in all its profundity. Many other jisei are dependent for their effect on knowledge of the circumstances in which they were composed. Here is one from early China by the master Beirei:

All Patriarchs are above our understanding,
And they don't last forever.
O my disciples, examine, examine.
What? Why this. This only.

Beirei exhorts his followers to examine the only thing worthy of their awareness, oneself in the here and now, 'this' of the last line. Attempting to understand the Patriarchs, Scripture, etc., distracts from real issues on the meditative path. The objection, generally, to such learning in the Zen community is that it inevitably leads to presuppositions concerning the nature of the world, those of others, whereas meditation may lead to insight into the very heart of things, a world not tampered by philosophy.

From its birth Zen Buddhism saw the necessity of creating conditions which might lead to personal salvation, as sought by generations of Taoists long before Bodhidharma, Zen's first patriarch, left India for China in the sixth century. They had been inspired by Lao Tzu, Taoism's founder, and his most illustrious follower, Chuang Tzu, to break free of the social and moral constraints of Confucianism, and were considered anarchic. Yet when Taoism anchored itself in

Buddhism, and thus became Zen, it acquired order and tremendous purpose, even spiritual transcendence. Here, a poem by Ikuzanshu:

I was born with a divine jewel,
Long since filmed with dust.
This morning, wiped clean, it mirrors
Streams and mountains, without end.

Enlightenment, sudden, miraculous (it is said that the master gained satori when, crossing. a bridge, he was thrown by his donkey), is spiritual cleansing, a return to the purity of Original Self, of which the jewel is a common symbol. Another way of seeing Ikuzanshu's poem is that, as a natural Taoist, he was indeed born with a divine jewel, but lacking the discipline of a path like Zen allowed it to 'film with dust'. With the achievement of Zen's greatest prize, satori, the world was transformed.

When in the twelfth century Zen reached Japan it quickly attracted influential leaders, who saw its discipline as full of possibilities for training followers, and thus became a great force. But its most distinguished masters were wary of such associations and patterned themselves and their temples on the most austere Chinese models. They even wrote in Chinese, and there is a oneness in their poems with those of their Chinese contemporaries. But soon masters like Dogen, of the thirteenth century, began using their own language and the established Japanese poetic forms. Here is one of the great master Dogen's early poems:

This slowly drifting cloud is pitiful;
What dreamwalkers men become.
Awakened, I hear the one true thing –
Black rain on the roof of Fukakusa Temple.

And here, years later, is his death poem:

Four and fifty years
I've hung the sky with stars.
Now I leap through –
What shattering!

Another jisei, by Dogen's thirteenth-century contemporary, Doyu:

Fifty-six years, above Buddhas, Patriarchs,
I've stood mid-air.
Now I announce my final journey –
Daily sun breaks from the eastern ridge.

Thus like the sun itself, which daily comes and goes, the poet came
and must leave, after a life of standing mid-air in contemplative withdrawal. It is remarkable that men who did not make a practice of
writing poetry, certainly did not think thenmselves poets, could at
critical moments find it within themselves to compose masterly works.

A few more death poems of the Japanese masters:

These eight-four years,
Still, astir, Zen's been mine.
My last work?
Spoken before time began.

— Kangan, 1217–1300

One thousand and one tumbles,
Ninety-one years through.
Snow covers reeds for miles,
Full in the midnight sky, the moon.

— Tetsu, 1219–1309

Drop by drop, seventy-seven winters,
Water's turned to ice.
Now this miraculous stroke –
I draw water from the flaming fount.

— Keso, 1352–1428

At all times conscious of examples they were setting, full of desire to
guide disciples well beyond their earthly term, and continue in living
memory, the Zen masters of China and Japan, and wherever else the
discipline established itself, achieved the miracle of perfect art. A final
word should be left to Kokan (1770–1843), who not only accepted
nearing death with calm and a touch of humour, but respected it for
the mystery it will always be:

For seventy-four years
I've touched east, west.
My parting word?
Listen – I'll whisper.

Photography

FERGUS ALLEN

Drink Me

Advertising photographs are at the opposite pole to press photographs: while the latter show us the world as it is, and often as we wish it were not, the former present us with the world as advertisers believe we would like it to be and as they aim to convince us that we think and have always thought it should be.

In *Decoding Advertisements* (Marion Boyars, 1978), Judith Williamson analysed the functioning of advertisements and the ideologies within which she saw them as working, but in so far as there were photographic images in the examples she considered – and in the most of them there were – her interest was in their message-bearing properties and the meanings they appropriated rather than in their characteristics and quality as photographs. She was concerned with the way in which advertisements seek to entangle us in systems of values that we come to take as 'given' and that, being accepted unawares, determine our patterns of spending in ways advantageous to the advertisers. But the photographs themselves deserve a closer look. In the first place they reflect the availability of money for still photography in quantities that are unknown outside military circles or the exploration of space – money for advanced equipment of the highest quality, for the most refined materials, the most precise and reliable processing, and for whatever labour and logistical support may be necessary to secure images that will command the market. Expensive, large-format cameras are needed to produce the finely grained negatives that, as well as being in exquisitely sharp focus, are of such a size that they do not have to be enlarged many times for publication. This is a realm of planning and deliberation and experiment, where cameras stand on tripods and reflected and incident light are carefully metered, and where shots are repeated until every shadow, pleat of skirt and strand of hair is satifactorily placed within the frame and in relation to every other element of the picture.

If the strategy of the advertising director requires visions of the tropics, off go the photographer and his models and assistants and paraphernalia to Kenya or the Leeward Islands. Locally engaged carriers hump the lighting stands and booms and the crates of refrigerated professional film from place to place, while technicians guard the precious cameras and lenses. On site, the allowances to be paid for subsistence and overtime mount up as the team waits for unseasonal cloud to disperse. But at last the weather looks right and everyone jumps to it. To save on film would be a false economy, but if cash is short the models may have to apply their own cosmetics. The assistants move obediently to the photographer's orders, handing him the newly loaded cameras and holding up reflectors or shades as directed, here to throw a diffused light on an overshadowed eye or neck and there to cancel an unwanted glitter. From this pose to that the models shift, adjusting their expressions as required to suggest desire, hauteur or menace; the sun moves, shadows grow shorter and a dust-devil wavers across the scrub in the middle distance (this, caught by luck in the background of a contrived scene, makes the image that will head the new campaign). But the shooting goes on. After dark the children in a nearby village are kept awake by the portable generator that powers the photofloods – flashlight would be too harsh for this delicate assignment. Roll after roll of film gets exposed. Then the packing for home and departure by night. Who are all those silent people on the roof of the airport terminal at two in the hot humid morning, what do they expect to see? And here is the huge spotlit aircraft, gleaming on the apron, surviving under the artificial respiration of roaring air-conditioners until the moment when it can drag itself into the still dark sky. Announcements in two languages, whisky, champagne cocktails, tissues impregnated with chilled cologne, instructions about life-jackets, what is called the sophisticated West. And in the hold, all those latent images, some of which will help to sell more tyres or rum or cigarettes.

Or perhaps the photographer has been engaged to publicize the attractions of a career in the Army. Here Alan Brooking describes how he set up a costly *mise en scène*:

'After a location hunt across Salisbury Plain by helicopter, I asked for six tanks to be at a certain map reference an hour before dawn. We drove down from London in the small hours to be ready for their arrival . . . I arranged three tanks in the foreground and had the other three rush up and down . . . to kick up a dust haze over what I could see was going to be a really brassy dawn. Behind me, and up-wind, the account executive was setting off smoke candles to create a white mist low down through the scene.'

If what is wanted is a puzzle-picture, a fantasy, a facetious essay in popular surrealism or something that would be called dreamlike, it may be just a matter of arranging and photographing a bizarre conjunction of subjects (a dishwasher in a ploughed field, perhaps), but for some advertisements elaborate sets have to be constructed and optical illusions recorded. Parts of different pictures – all of them specially taken – may have to be juxtaposed or assembled as a photomontage, each more or less in photographic accord with the adjacent parts. To carry conviction, the photographs that are combined must have comparable ranges of tone or colour, the joins must not show when the composition has been rephotographed, and if behind the main three-dimensional subject a slide of scenery (mountains in Arizona, for example) is projected on a screen, it should not be identifiable as a photographic backdrop in the final image. All this calls for elaborate apparatus, craftsmanship, time and money. (Despite their borrowed surrealistic clothes, it is not easy to classify these pictures. They are not paintings or drawings, but, although making them involves two or even three stages of photography, neither are they

Photo Fergus Allen

photographs in the usual sense. Perhaps they are best placed as devitalized relatives of the collages made by artists like Duchamp, Ernst and Kurt Schwitters in the Twenties and Thirties. But this does not reduce their effectiveness as advertisements.)

More interesting than its financial aspect is the advertising photograph's misrepresentaional role. Suppose that a manufacturer and his publicity agent agree that an advertisement for ice-cream should include a photograph of a scoopful of that ice-cream in the pink of condition in a sundae glass. Given the depth of field required, and therefore the aperture at which he will have to work and the intensity of the illumination that will be necessary, the photographer knows that real ice-cream would start to melt as soon as he switched on the lamps. As he has not been commissioned to supply a picture of half-melted ice-cream, he must look around for a substance which, perhaps after some titivation, will yield a photographic image closely resembling that which the ice-cream at its most enticing would have yielded but for the technical difficulties. It may be that freshly mixed plaster of Paris will serve this purpose, or mashed potato given a faint shine with a breath from an aerosol spray of hair lacquer. Whatever the substitute, imagine the photograph taken and the colourful mouth-watering image on the page of a glossy magazine. There are then two possibilities: either the representation may be in the opinion of a panel of impartial witnesses be indistinguishable from the reality, or it may be more alluring and appetizing

(the alternative of its being less so may be ruled out, because in that case the picture would be suppressed).

The photograph in the advertisement will not have an explicit identifying title or caption stating that the picture is a faithful portrayal of a sample of such-and-such a brand of ice-cream. The text may evoke the delights of cool refreshment at times of heat and drought, and it may be hinted that a shared sundae is a natural precursor to a night of love; there may also be references to the nutritional value of ice-cream and the strict standards of hygience maintained in its preparation; but nowhere will it be said that the accompanying illustration is a photographic image of the substance with these properties that is made and sold by the company whose name is displayed prominently above or below. The deception is oblique. The picture is shown in proximity to words about ice-cream, and it is left to the viewer to infer if he wishes that the former depicts the latter. But if this were put forward as a line of defence against a charge of fraudulent description, it would be open to rejection on the grounds that it would be reasonable for any person of common sense to make the connection.

If the supposed ice-cream in the photograph looks more attractive than the real thing seen under similar illumination in a similar dish or glass, the viewer – subsequently the buyer – can fairly claim to have been misled as far as the appearance, though not of course the taste, was concerned. But if the picture gives a true impression of the real ice-cream's appearance, it follows that the look of the product cannot fall short of the viewer's expectations – and to this extent he will not have been misled. The deception, such as it is, consists in leading him to think that a photograph of, say, lightly glazed and tinted mashed potato is a photograph of ice-cream. He may go to his grave without realizing the error into which he has been encouraged to fall. However, if the photographer is accused of falsification, he can argue that he was obliged to perpetrate the lie in order to convey the visual truth. The mashed potato was no more than a means of showing what that make of ice-cream looked like. It might have been done by commissioning a realistic painting of the ice-cream and then photographing the painting and reproducing it. In that case would it be morally objectionable if the model for the painting had been mashed potato rather than ice-cream? The nub of the this apparent problem lies in the widespread assumption – a tacit assumption on which the advertiser can safely bank – that every photograph is an optically unmistakable image of its objective correlative. This is not an assumption that we make about even the most seemingly representational painting, because we know that the painter and his imagination and his unique nervous system and musculature have necessarily intervened between the subject and the picture of that subject.

While it may be out of the ordinary for one substance to be used to simulate another for photographic purposes, it does not follow that all is completely above board when an apple poses as an apple and an hotel bedroom as a bedroom in that same hotel. In advertising, the emphasis is on those qualities of whatever is being promoted that the maker and the advertising agent believe will take the fancy of potential buyers. Some of these qualities – the aural, olfactory and kinetic, for example – have to be treated in words, but those which photographs can deal with include the visible features of design, superficial finish or texture, size (large or small), location, shape and colour, each of which, when related to the merchandise or service on offer, will make its contribution to the advertisement's message.

Taking as an instance the illustrations that publicize hotels in brochures about holidays, a camera with a standard lens cannot encompass enough of a typical bedroom to produce a picture that will inform and make a favourable impression on a viewer planning his vacation. However, a photograph taken through a wide-angle lens, as well as doing what is required in showing more of the room, will also, from its inherent perspective, have the convenient property of causing it to appear considerably larger than a person entering the room would find it to be. The picture cannot be said to be false, because a viewer with normal sight would get a 'normal' impression if he held it at about half the ordinary reading distance from his eyes (given that he were able to focus on it at the shorter range). This quality of amplitude in photographs taken with wide-angle lenses is naturally exploited by advertisers to represent certain spaces or volumes as being less confined than they actually are. A familiar application is in advertisements for motor cars, where what you understood to be a small saloon is shown as an imposing presence before a Palladian facade, while obviously affluent men and women lounge contentedly inside it. There is no need to suppose the existence of a miniature bourgeoisie, specially bred for these pictures. It can all be done by wide-angle lenses and the careful relative placement of people, cars and buildings.

The most daunting quality of life in the advertised world is its perfection. The women's faces are immaculate (spotless), clothes have creases and folds only where they are intended to be creased and folded, pots and pans glitter and birds do not shit on the garden furniture. It is a world without fingerprints, smears, mud, grit, grease-stains, floating hairs and fluff. The objects in it are not scratched, chipped, cracked, torn or faded; the yolks of eggs are unbroken and no black specks sully their whites. Elegantly dressed, radiating masculine potential or womanly receptivity, the moderate smokers are unaffected by emphysema. Technologically advanced machinery responds, quickly and precisely, when well groomed male fingers play confidently over bewildering panels of switches. The weather is either sunny or dramatically, photogenically bad.

The scenes owe their unreal, dreamlike air to the elimination of time, the absence of any signs of growth, development or decay. In this living-room or that kitchen nothing has ever changed and presumably never will; nothing happens, except for trivial incidents like the spilling of a few drops of liqueur on the white carpet or of cooking oil on the thermoplastic tiles, which can of course be rectified with a wipe of the advertised detergent, whereupon everything is exactly as it was before. The compliments on the coffee, the judicious evaluations of the sherry and the admiring comments on the efficacy of the washing powder will be repeated indefinitely, with the same twinkles, pursings and round-eyed wonder. That smiling, grey-haired, crinkly person – the euphemistic symbol of old age – can never be or have been anything but smiling, grey-haired and crinkly. Rising peach-like from a night's sleep, the enchantress stands stretching her lovely limbs beside a disordered bed, sheets and blankets tossed aside or sprigged duvet grotesquely rumpled – but it is a composed, arranged disorder. Tomorrow morning she will be equally dewy, her nightdress will still look freshly ironed and her background will be untidied in just the same deliberately picturesque way. The accidental and contingent are ruled out, the spider suspends its operations.

Time is admitted – but only under strict instructions to behave itself – when experience, endurance, stability and continuity are attributes to be associated with the subject of the advertisement. Banks and building societies like to be thought of in these terms. It is then okay to depict castles, cathedrals and old manor-houses with flaking masonry, crumbling mortar and twisted sun-bleached timbers. But the weathering cannot be more than superficial; it must be evident to the dimmest viewer that the structures are good for many centuries to come. And if ancient trees or Chelsea pensioners are allowed on stage, they too should be seen to have a fair number of years ahead of them.

Usually, however, advertisements are intended not to assure the public about conditions years ahead, but to speak to them about the appearance and action of things in the near future. Then the stress is always on the new, the flawless, the spick and span. In these beguiling pictures the wares seem superior in form and colour to the comparable objects that the viewer is accustomed to use or consume. This, runs the implicit message, is how they ought to look, this is the image of quality. But persuading buyers to judge by appearances can have odd consequences. Not only do goods tend to become esteemed for their photogenic properties – because they lend themeselves to the making of striking colour photographs – but situations may arise where they are actually designed or bred to have these properties, even if this entails the loss of others that are more important. Some of the tastiest varieties of strawberry have relatively small, often mishapen berries, with greyish or greenish patches among the red, whose goodness is recognized by the nose and tongue rather than the eye. Eating is what they are grown for. But if more reliably heart-shaped fruit of two or three times the size and a uniform glossy scarlet would make more eye-catching photographs, the plant breeders can develop them and do. And the pictures duly tempt the public to buy and go on buying what prove to be insipid, watery berries. The lesson is learned so slowly, and the spell of the images is so strong, that by the time people have cottoned on to what is happening, market gardeners are producing only the gaudy inferior fruit and the more primitive varieties are hard to find.

Advertising photographers do much more than simply inform the public about the functions, characteristics and prices of the various goods and services on sale. Of Alan Brooking, for example, it was said that 'he creates images which aim to influence your thoughts and deeds'. Influence is the 'power of producing an effect, especially unobtrusively' and 'ascendancy, often of a secret or undue kind'. With an advertisement defined as 'any device for obtaining public favour or notoriety', we get the impression of someone whose purpose, veiled or not, is to induce us to do or acquire something that we should probably not otherwise have done or acquired, first and foremost for his and his client's benefit rather than ours. The photographer's task in an advertising campaign is to provide the visual elements of a fantasy, or rather some stills around which the viewer, helped by the printed word, will be led to construct the intended fantasy. The pictures may be imaginative essays or concoctions put together for our entertainment, to soften us up for the commercial message, or they may be idealized depictions of aspects of the working world we know, but either way their purpose is to make us discontented with our possessions and our present way of living. Unless we feel that discontent we shall not buy the easy-to-grip hair-dryer with unique safety cut-out, the jumbo-size tube of striped toothpaste, the off-peak economy-class ticket, the fully lined natural silk suit, the domesticated mini-computer (with which to calculate the interest due to us on our inflation-linked investments), or the kit from which we can assemble a solid hardwood long-case clock with Westminster chime and Tempus Fugit dial. At this point the advertising photographer will defend himself against accusations that he prostitutes his craft by drawing our attention to his essential role in the business that keeps money on the move, commerce and industry active and prevents unemployment from being even worse than it is. But from this flow arguments that have little to do with photography.

There are classes of objects, activities and causes other than the profitably commercial that still photographs are used to advertise. One of these is the work of charitable organisations. Being charities, they cannot risk being regarded as spendthrift, so it is usual for published photographs of the destitute, the starving, the malformed and diseased to be technically indifferent and in black and white. Printed in slightly blurred greys, the image of a chair-bound boy with muscular dystrophy reminds us not only of the distressful condition of the group of unfortunate people he represents, but directly, through its inferior quality, of the absence of the funds needed to improve that condition. The poverty of the picture underlines the pathos of the subject. Whereas the photographs used in commercial advertising appeal to us as status and pleasure-seekers, this one aims to make us suffer – by inducing fears for our own well-being and guilt and pity on behalf of the afflicted – and simultaneously to offer the means of relieving that suffering by contributing cash to the organisation that placed the advertisement.

Financial considerations apart, if the picture of the crippled boy were in colour, subtly lit, in needle-sharp focus, taken with all the technical support and finesse that is available for advertising chocolate or hi-fi equipment, would it be more effective in raising money? Probably not, because the more incisive photograph would, by illustrating the discomfort, disablement and abnormality of the child's condition so vividly, concentrate the mind on the plight of this particular but unnamed boy rather than on the situation of the hundreds or thousands of incapacitated people in whose interest he has been photographed. What is wanted is a touching symbol, not a brilliantly harrowing portrayal of the individual case, and this the second-rate black-and-white picture provides.

Closely related are the illustrated advertisements for minor cults and religions. Some consist of indistinct pictures of buildings of indeterminate age – domes, places of worship or physically based spiritual exercise – but these are outnumbered by full-face photographs of the organisations' founders or leaders – partially undressed Indians sitting with their legs uncomfortably crossed, or spectacled men (men, not women) whose insight into the human condition is indicated by the intensity with which they stare at the lens. Whether the advertiser adopts a hard-selling line or plays it softly, new members and their subscriptions and donations are what he is after, and with such an aim it would not be surprising if he used more alluring pictures. But although these sects and their leaders are often affluent in more than spirit, photographs of the quality associated with high-grade commercial advertisements would smack too strongly of this world and its bank balances.

This was certainly not the attitude that the Christian Church took to quality when it commissioned pictures before the invention of photography. These paintings may be indisputable works of art, as well as being imbued with religious feeling, but they are also, and perhaps primarily, advertisements for the Christian faith issued on behalf of, say, the Roman Catholic Church. Inside or outside consecrated buildings, in oil or tempera or fresco, the countless renderings of the Annunciation, the Nativity, the Madonna and Child, the Crucifixion, the Deposition and other events from the New Testament, together with innumerable martyrdoms, are the remains of what must have been the most powerful and sustained advertising campaign the West has ever seen. In them art was very much the servant of a multinational religious corporation. Though it may not have been laid down for him in so many words, the painter's task was to 'sell' this religion to the viewer, just as the advertising photographer's is to persuade him to seek the consolation of certain brands of whisky or vitamin pill.

Whether, in the years when they were establishing themselves and later when they were dominant, photography could have served the Greek or Roman Churches – or Buddhism – as effectively as it does the brewers and oil companies today may be a hypothetical and historically meaningless question. If there were now to be a sequence of events analogous to those that occurred in the neighbourhood of Nazareth, Bethlehem and Jerusalem two thousand years ago, it seems on the face of it unlikely that they would have analogous consequences. But, putting history aside, if the Stations of the Cross or the principal events of the Christian calendar had been recorded by skilful press photographers and the results enlarged and distributed far and wide, would they have been as influential as the paintings that helped inspire and uphold the faith over centuries? If we assume, as we must, that the photographic image of Jesus would have had the characteristics of a man and not those of a superman or supernatural being, the probability is that they would not. A mystery cannot be successfully propagated by uncovering even a corner of that mystery. Paintings, however naturalistic in style, depict Jesus as in some respect transcending or being metaphorically larger than life; photographs could only record the image of the human envelope in which we are told He manifested himself. There is no reason to suppose that ordinary photographic emulsions are any more sensitive to the ineffable than they are to the invisible. With the tricks of their trade, painters could symbolize or hint at the numinous power that underlay His words, actions and prescence; but not the photographers. They might capture pictures of a man addressing large or small groups of people, supposedly healing the sick, being publicly humiliated or clearly in great suffering, but other people have performed ostensibly similar actions or undergone similar trials, and photographs taken of then doing so have not aroused more than interest, sympathy or a consciousness of injustice, which is less than a Church Militant would require of its advertising agents. And while a caption would increase the interest of such a photograph by providing informantion (true or untrue) about the circumstances, it would not increase its emotional impact. At a more everyday level, for example, a picture of a bearded man haranguing a crowd, whom we have taken to be an ineffectual orator at Hyde Park Corner, acquires a new importance when we learn that it is a photograph of Lenin. However, though the image that we only glanced at before may now hold our attention, it does not do much to advance the cause of Marxist-Leninism, which is – or was – better done by idealized paintings.

Hairdressing

BILLIE LYDIA PORTER

Elmo

'Your name?' she says looking up at me with eyes a shade of turquoise that only contact lenses can create, and her scrambled masses of yellow hair shudder as she moves her head. Her eyes pierce mine and wait.

'Lydia,' I force myself to say. 'Lydia Howard.' My eyes escape to watch her draw a black line through my name. How quickly she dispenses with it; its meaning now is gone. I think of it there in her big rumpled book; waiting on the white desk for the real Me to render it nil. I think of it in the dark, at night, when the shop was closed and no one saw it at all. I think of the book opened in the day, exposed to anybody's view, but know it was not really noticed among the scribble of names that never fit the tiny little boxes laid in rows. I feel better now, somehow, my name is back with me.

She thrusts a rolled-up garment at me, and her heavy garish rings slide loosely around her long thin fingers. 'You can change in the dressing-room behind you. Elmo will be ready when you come out.'

Her attempt at sophistication fails and her attitude is merely perfunctory, but it expects no personal connection and that suits me just fine. I want none from her; it would be an intrusion. I escape to the dresssing-room with relief, glad to be away from the long white counters and cabinets, the gleaming chrome and leather chairs, the bustle of the hairdressers snipping and combing, the whirring of dryers fluffing newly-cut hair, and, worst of all, the double expanse of mirrors filling both the walls from the front to the back of the shop. The dressing-room has a mirror too, but I ignore it as I hang my coat and put the kimono on and tie the sash. The one-size-fits-all wraps double around my waist and looks anything but chic, but I don't care. I like the colour, it is grey.

Out again into the lighted room, I discover Elmo waiting for me. He starts to smile, and then haltingly says, 'This way please, and I will wash your hair.' Elmo is fat. There could be nicer ways to say it, but it's true. Unlike the other male hairdressers in the room, whose shirts are voluminous and hide their slim bodies except in the front where they reveal gold chains or curling hairs, his shirt strains to reach around his body, and just barely holds on by the security of the buttons.

I sit in the chair and lean back, with my neck pressed uncomfortably into the cold porcelain edge of the sink. He begins his lathered scrubbing and bobs my head around and makes my neck hurt more. His short, stubby fingers work furiously over my scalp. I close my eyes and try to think it is lovely and feels like being pampered, but the hasty vigour with which he works make that impossible. I remember, instead, that my mother used to attack my head the same way when I was a child. She had thick, strong fingers too, and they had

no gentleness in them, though they only ever struck me once. I hated the sight of them; they were fat and shiny, but her compulsive washing never made the freckles fade. I remember the last time I saw her, just two days before she died. The cancer had wasted her corpulence to less than ninety pounds, but her hands still looked the same. She was so weak she couldn't lift her head from the pillow, but she reached for my son's hands to grasp, and held them very tight.

Suddenly a lever on my chair is pushed and I am sitting up. Elmo wraps a towel around my head and swirls it expertly into a twist that will pull the water from my hair. Together we walk across the gleaming floor whose polished wood is nearly the same shade as the hair of the receptionist. I wonder is she had dyed it to match. I settle into the chair while Elmo waits and watches me in the mirror. I do not look at him.

'How do you want it this time? Same as before?' he asks, drawing the comb through the tangles with swift little pulling motions.

'Yes, it was fine,' I say. 'Really fine. You may do it just the same.'

The woman on my left is getting a cut, but I watch, instead, the woman on my right. The hairdresser is separating out tiny strips of her long hair and applying little squares of foil to the roots that he paints with something and then painstakingly folds the foil, leaving long strands hanging down. I am curious and ask Elmo what is going on, but I don't think he understands me and he mutters something I don't understand in reply. He is Italian, and his accent mangles his words. I marvel at how the women stare with fixed absorption at their images on the wall. I wonder what they think, as they look at themselves, and I wait to catch them preen. The idea of it fascinates me so; but I feel embarrassed for them as I watch. Perhaps I am unkind, to think it strange to stare at oneself. Maybe it's because it's something I can no longer do.

The image I see when I look in the mirror is someone I don't know. The person who stares back at me is someone from another life, where there was meaning and belonging and love, and now there is none. There is no one now to care how well my hair is cut, or to marvel at the fineness of its sheen. I get it cut when I can no longer make it to fall the way it should.

'Is this short enough?' says Elmo, pulling the front piece down to the level of my jaw.

'Yes,' I say, 'that's fine.' But I wish it could be longer, so it would cover more. I want to obliterate the person I see; I want to be invisible. I don't want anyone else to see that person either, or to talk, as talking breaks the wall. I need the wall, as I have no context now. I am not part of Life, and need it to protect what there is left of Me, as I am all there is.

In the mirror I see the receptionist risking her way across the shiny floor in her five-inch heels. She looks defenceless out from behind her desk, and even thinner than I thought. The blousey black jumpshirt she wears is pulled in by a wide cinch belt around a waist that can barely be twenty inches. She is tall, and the combination of the stilted movements of her stick-like body and the huge mass of tangled hair around her painted face make her seem a caricature of a scarecrow in a field.

'Your wife called,' she addresses Elmo, 'she says you'll have to pick up the kids; she's gonna be staying late at work.'

Elmo grunts a reply, and continues working on my hair. I look briefly at him in the mirror and suddenly he's a Person. He has a context. He has a wife, and I wonder what she's like. What is there about him that she loves? I see limp hair parted and combed long over his early-balding forehead, and a pasty, pudgy face. It is a passionless face, and one that never changes, even when he smiles. I wonder if he feels things, and think he surely must; he has children, after all.

I look at the woman to my left. She is clearly preening now, as her hair is nearly done. I wonder what she is thinking as she looks in the mirror. Does she look so different she has to get to know herself again? I doubt that. I think, instead, she is looking at herself as 'he' will look at her, and is trying to judge what he will see. She looks pleased; there is anticipation in her look. I look away again.

Will this process never end? Will he never finish so I can get away from the reflection of myself two feet away? The woman to my left is done and leaving now. The woman to my right is far from done. Her head, a mass of tinfoil squares with long hair trailing down, I am like the sculpture of a not-quite inspired artist in an insignificant museum of modern art. I am still curious, but I guess I'll never know what she is doing to her hair. Elmo isn't likely to suggest such a thing to me.

'Do you want spray?' he asks now, as he combs my hair in place.

'No, thank you,' I say, trying not to let feelings edge my words, 'I have nowhere special to go tonight, I am only going home.'

Without a word, he takes off the cape and turns my chair around. He has not offered the hand mirror, and I assume he knows I do not care to look. Suddenly the wall I'd built dissolves; I see I've cheated him. I have left my own world for an hour, and entered into his. I have an obligation that till now I have withheld. I pay the receptionist, and return to the chair with his tip. As I hand it to him I do my best to smile and meet his eyes with mine.

'Thank you,' I say, 'it does look very nice.'

I turn and escape to the door, glad to be outside. The wind quickly takes the smoothness of my hair and tangles it at will. I let it blow and do not care; I need the wind's caress.

Opera

GREGORY STRONG

My Debut in the Chinese Opera

I made my debut in the Chinese Opera after sightseeing in Chengdu city in Sichuan, China. I met a certain Mr Lee. For a small charge, he could not only arrange a ticket for an opera, but also a backstage tour. 'I know the director,' he confided in me. And then Mr Lee offered me a chance to appear on stage. 'At no extra cost,' he added quickly, taking my arm.

'Every visitor to China sees the fabulous Chinese Opera,' said the diminutive Mr Lee. 'Singing, dancing, *la pantomime,* even acrobatics!' We sat together in the Flower Garden Restaurant as he spoke enthusiastically about the Opera. 'Classics like "Picking Up a Jade Bracelet", or "Su San, A Wronged Prostitute".'

'Let me get this straight,' I said, 'I could actually appear in the opera?' Mr Lee nodded vigorously. 'But I can't sing in Chinese,' I protested. That didn't seem to matter, so I added, 'I'm only visiting Chengdu for a few days.' That didn't seem to matter, either, so at last I capitulated, and handed over a few dollars. 'I can do a pretty fair handstand,' I suggested.

Several acquaintances staying at my hotel joined me for a matinée performance at a crumbling third-rate opera-house. The toilets were in a red brick outhouse in the yard. Inside the theatre, 300 to 400 patrons in quilted jackets were already seated. Or perhaps I should say already snoring, because most of the audience were pensioners, and they had slumped over in their chairs and were sound asleep.

They were sheltering from the wind outside, as much as they were there to see opera. I thought the lighting in the theatre was dim. The floorboards creaked and the stage was covered in a tattered, patched blue curtain. It was a very modest venue.

However, there is a glamour to every theatre, and so with this one. Once I had trodden on that threadbare stage, the threshold between the actors and their audience, the magic began. The actors had drifted backstage in grey street clothes, and poorly cut jackets, and the women in navy blazers, black trousers, and cloth shoes. But then their transformation began. They put on make-up. Old women lost their wrinkles. Plain women acquired flushed cheeks, and rosebud lips. Thin-faced young men gained lines of character, and experience. Paunchy, middle-aged men with doughy features acquired square jaws, and grand, trumpeting eyebrows.

'You are all going to be in the opera,' announced Mr Lee as we sat behind the curtain. His arms were behind his back. He paced back and forth before us. 'You will all be made up.'

Would I ever get another chance to appear in a Chinese Opera? So how could I refuse the opportunity? I was joined by an Australian elementary school teacher, and a Japanese salaryman visiting China from Tokyo. The three of us were made up.

One of the actresses smeared a kind of colourless grease onto my face, then white, black, and pink pigment, with a cherry red for my lips.

With my thick black eyebrows, and moustache, I imagined that I'd look like some kind of fierce Japanese kabuki-style actor. I could hardly wait to see myself in a mirror. But on first glance, I looked a trifle effeminate. Such pink cheeks and red lips! And a mark on my cheek looked suspiciously like a beauty spot. What exactly was I going to play here?

Nervously, I watched the stage hands prepare to raise the curtain. Mr Lee sat chatting amicably with the director. I interrupted them. 'What do I do here?' I asked.

'You?' said Mr. Lee. 'You will play a soldier.' He turned to the other foreigners. 'You will all play soldiers.' He gave us no idea of what we were supposed to do but he marched across the stage in a quick pantomime of how we were to enter.

'But what do I do on stage?' I asked in exasperation.

'Why, nothing,' said Mr Lee. 'You just stand there.'

I thought I could do that well enough so I spent the next few minutes practising my entrance. I bowed formally, and ceremonially, at centre stage, as do all characters entering the stage in an opera piece. Then I assumed a martial stance at a position beside the throne at centre-stage. The actor playing the Prime Minister in the piece was to be seated on the throne with his army and servants lined up nearly on either side of him.

I soon found the Prime Minister. He was a snaggle-toothed little man with a monkey's face.

Rolling his hips, he was performing an elaborate little dance before a few of the other male actors.

I marched past with another soldier. I am sure he winked at me. I thought about switching armies.

Then all of a sudden, there was a last minute change in the parts we were going to play. I lost my part! The blonde

Australian school teacher got it. She and the Japanese salaryman would play the soldiers because they were the same height. Oh, that maddening Chinese preoccupation with symmetry! I thought to myself.

'What about me?' I asked. 'What do I play, Mr Lee? – Captain of the guard?' I suggested hopefully.

'You?' said Mr Lee. 'You will be a servant.'

'A servant!' I said. So much for my debut. I considered pulling out of the show or striking for a better role among the actors. But then only they knew how to remove my make-up. And I certainly didn't want to walk the streets like this. I consoled myself with the thought that I would be a high-ranking servant in the Imperial court. Or if I wasn't really of high rank, I would imagine myself to be of high rank.

The actors and actresses in the company began pulling down these huge trunks of costumes from shelves backstage. Although the theatre might be a very humble one, the costumes we were to wear were magnificent. In Chinese theatre, the leading actors and actresses get the most beautiful robes. So the Prime Minister got a splendid silk gown with dragons on it.

The general, a roly-poly old man with a loose set of false teeth, who was standing there in his undershirt, got a fine helmet, and a matching gown with padded shoulders, and black boots with lifts in them. When he'd put on his costume, he suddenly looked tall and handsome, even fierce and war-like.

The two other tourists got rich-looking royal blue gowns with gold dragons on them. Did I say all the costumes were magnificent? Just when my hopes were up, I was handed a flimsy blue wrap. It looked like a cotton bathrobe. In compensation perhaps, I was also given one of those remarkable opera hats that look like coal scuttles with Christmas bulbs sticking from them. Next, I received a horsehair tassel. Was it to ward off the flies settling on the Prime Minister?

With minutes left before curtain time, we still didn't know what the play was that we were supposed to be doing. At the very last moment, Mr Lee told us the play was about an old emperor who was tricked into giving up his position to an ambitious and unscrupulous Prime Minister. Good casting, I thought to myself. I didn't trust the Prime Minister, either.

It seemed to me that the story was going to be pretty simple. My time on stage would be spent listening to somebody express his emotions at the awful turn of events. Sort of like the Greek plays I had read in school. One long tragedy. But what was beginning to worry me was that I'd heard of Chinese operas lasting as long as six hours.

'Just exactly how long are we supposed to be onstage, Mr Lee?' I asked. I expected a cameo role like the walk-on parts for bit players in the Western theatre.

'For the whole performance.'

I'd forgotten that I'd often heard of huge casts onstage in Chinese Operas. Now I understood why. There are no sets in a Chinese opera so the fifteen of us onstage had to represent the Emperor's entire palace. In practice, this meant that all the Imperial supernumeraries – maids-in-waiting, lieutenants, captains, soldiers, and yes, even servants – stood on the stage for the whole performance. Too late to leave now!

The curtain rose. We appeared. In walked the Imperial court and the principals. The Prime Minister, and the fierce general, drew a ripple of polite applause. I believe that much of the audience was still asleep. Still, like the other foreigners who filed onto the stage, I was taking my role very seriously. I'd even taken off my glasses to look like a more authentic court retainer. I took a deep bow. A crackle of laughter swept the audience. Regrettably, I'd forgotten to take off my running shoes.

Actually, I wish I could say that I kept them rolling in the aisles for the entire performance. Or for that matter, even awake. But a minute later, they'd slumped back into their seats in the crowded theatre. Lit cigarettes flickered in a few dozen places. Several people were eating apples. I suspect that someone had a transistor radio.

But I think that most of the audience had fallen back asleep.

Soon I wished I could have fallen asleep myself. The opera piece seemed interminable. The old emperor, doddering across the stage, sang some sad old song that every pensioner in the audience apparently knew. Some were even joining in. The ageing actor who played the part couldn't do any of the usual opera acrobatics. Instead of flips and somersaults to express great emotion, he only managed a few squats

on the stage. All the same, he had every sympathy from the audience. The greater he tried, and the less he did, the more he was appreciated. The pensioners in the audience knew what it meant to grow old, to lose their jobs.

Meanwhile I was standing to the left of the throne. I was finding it very hard to stand still for so long. I tried shifting my weight from one foot to another. But it didn't really help. I felt badly about ruining the performance until I noticed that several of the Chinese actors in minor parts were either coughing during the emperor's long speech or even leaving the stage to spit. Then the Australian teacher got dizzy, left the entourage, and fainted offstage. The performance was beginning to seem like an endurance test.

The only credible performer among us seemed to be the Japanese salaryman. 'I hate Tokyo,' he'd said to me earlier. So I guess he was used to suffering. I imagine he also was used to standing at staff meetings and listening to long harangues from the company's director.

In any case, there he stood, as mute, and expressionless, as if he were carved of wood.

In the meantime, I was trying to take my mind off things by considering whether an actor in the Chinese theatre approached his part as did a Western method actor. In other words, should I have 'an attitude' towards the old emperor? And should my attitude be expressed physically? Well, I was standing beside the Prime Minister so I was supposed to be on his side. I gave the emperor a hard look. This part was easy because I was getting so tired of standing onstage – Hurry up, and die, you old fool, I said to myself. Not surprisingly, I began to appreciate the Prime Minister for qualities I hadn't appreciated earlier. Yes, I thought to myself, what this empire needs is a new broom. We need a younger man with new ideas. At the very least, we need somebody who can get things done more quickly.

It was at this point that the general, wearing this magnificent helmet with two long ostrich plumes, began speaking, strutting up and down on the stage before me. He was upstaging me terribly. The other foreigners in our party were sitting in the front row and they began wildly snapping photographs of me.

It got worse than being upstaged. One of the general's feathers was bent and whenever he turned to make some remark to the Prime Minister, his crooked feather poked me in the face. The general kept waving his arms and clomping across the stage in his boots and I kept getting poked in the face. I tried squeezing my eyes shut. Then I tried tilting my head a bit to one side. It wasn't much good. Soon I began dipping from one side to the other. My friends in the audience started giggling. I tried to dodge the general's feather, inconspicuously, but I was almost doing calisthenics. Mr Leu and my friends in the audience were sitting in the front row and laughing uproariously.

Was it an hour? Or was it two? At last, the general switched sides, the ailing emperor collapsed, and the prime minister took the Imperial seal. There was applause and we trooped off stage. All the cast agreed afterward that the Japanese tourist had made the best actor. He'd been able to remain motionless for the entire performance. 'I hate Tokyo,' he said to me again backstage. I'd like to report that he was offered a permanent part with the opera troupe. But like the rest of us, his robes were whisked away. The curtain had fallen and a few singers had already taken our places for a boy-meets-girl story.

Mr Lee led us out of the theatre and into a brick-strewn alley where there was a concrete water trough. Before we bent over to wash off our make-up, we looked at each other's faces and we laughed. That was my debut in the Chinese Opera.

Theatre

FRANK McGUINNESS

Peacocks and Others

Shylock by John Gross (Chatto & Windus. £18)

Shylock is John Gross's rather meandering investigation into whether or not the character is anti-semitic, a question which might prompt the more irreverent to inquire if the Pope is a Catholic. Others might simply echo Gross's own quotation from *Anti-Semitism: The Longest Hatred* in which Robert Wistrich concludes that Shakespeare's portrait 'served to crystallize and reinforce an anti-semitic literary stereotype for centuries to come'. This robustly unequivocal judgement, of course, is at odds with other views represented in the book which exonerate the playwright from all taint of prejudice and even attempt to sell *The Merchant of Venice* as a satire on Christian tolerance. Nor does it wash with Gross, no less impervious that I, it would seem, to the subtle, tongue-in-cheek irony of such lines as 'I hate him for he is a Christian'. At least this would appear so from his final conclusion that Shylock is not only a figure cast very much in the mould of the Jew in Medieval European demonology, but has also played a significant part in fostering the prejudice leading up to the holocaust. However, the question he ducks is whether this suggests the play would have been better suppressed, or what we should do about John Patten's threat to introduce such a pernicious work into our schools and how we can prevent its falling into the hands of our servants.

In one respect, I must confess to having found *Shylock* something of an oddity in that I was never quite certain what sort of readership the author had in mind when writing it. As may be judged by the copious research, it was clearly intended as a serious work and yet, by its lack of originality and depth, it is hard to believe it would interest the genuine scholar, who would surely find much of the material commonplace. What is more, this becomes evident in the opening section of the work in which Gross, following what is rapidly becoming a tedious convention of all popular works on Shakespeare, leads off with a quick run-down on the origins of the play, precisely what was plagiarized by the dramatist, and the literary cross-fertilization that subsequently took place to give birth to the new product. Not that there is anything wrong with what Gross dutifully trots out about 'Il Pecorone' and 'The Ballad of Gernutus', any more than there is in his potted review of the respective merits of Shakespeare's play and Marlowe's *The Jew of Malta*. It is just that not even the most charitable critic could pretend that the passage offers anything more than might be gleaned from the average introduction to an A-level test.

The book becomes no more intellectually intriguing when Gross launches forth on some fanciful speculation about what may have prompted and influenced the dramatist in his work. At one point, for instance, he advances the notion that Shakespeare was less interested in Shylock as a Jew than as a moneylender, this interest stemming, it seems, from the playwright's own financial dealings which allowed him to 'understand the usurer from the inside'. Now I don't know if Will was an easy touch or what rate he charged, but the theory still strikes me as monumentally silly unless we are to assume that the average 17th-century moneylender was more interested in killing off a Christian than in turning over a quick ducat or two. But these reservations count little with Gross, particularly when he is able to call in support no less a person than James Joyce, himself the progenitor of a famous Jew. However, it seems that it was not Bloom himself but Stephen Dedalus who gave it as his opinion that Shakespeare 'drew Shylock out of his own long pocket', a view which so impresses Gross that he quotes it twice in the course of the book.

But if Gross invests this Joycean one-liner with more significance than is apparent to some of his readers, it has nothing on the quotation he lifts from Harold Fisch's 'The Dual Image' in consideration of how Jewish Shakespeare's Shylock really is. This reads: 'It is often said that in Shylock, Shakespeare penetrated into the psychology of the Jew . . . in his dark and gloomy resentments, his feverish care of his possessions, his sense of family . . . his loyalty to his fellow Jews, his love of his daughter, his gestures, his faith in the absolute validity of the written bond . . . his appeal to law against sentiment.'

Now this seems to me so foolish a comment that one can only wonder at Gross's lack of judgement in not only citing it in the first place, but also dubbing it an example of brilliant insight. All this might be true of Shylock and a good many more Jews as well. What I would question, however, is the implication that these traits are any more exclusively semitic than the features more commonly attributed to the Jew. The truth is that, give or take a word or two, the description would as easily fit a few Mancuniian Methodists I've met in my time, and probably not a few West Indian Baptists also.

If Gross's book lacks specialist intellectual clout, it is also rather too sober and uncontroversial a work to excite the layman. It may be true, as Gross argues, that Shylock is a familiar figure to millions who have never read or seen *The Merchant of Venice* but I doubt if this will lead to any great interest in seeing how the character has evolved over the last four hundred years.

Perhaps not so surprisingly for an inveterate compiler, whose previous two books were both collections, the first of anecdotes, the other of essays, Gross now comes up with what in large part adds up to a third collection (or perhaps *catalogue* is a better word) this time of the major Shylocks who have graced, or disgraced, the stage over the last four centuries. The list extends from Burbage – if, indeed, it was he who originated the role and not the low comedian, Will Kempe, playing the part, as was customary at the time with stage Jews, for laughs – right up to the 1987 Royal Shakespearean production which, during the Trial Scene, had Antonio tied to a pole while Shylock, in the guise of Anthony Sher, swooped on him like a demented bird of prey, all the time chanting Hebraic spells. In short, also played for laughs.

The trouble with catalogues, however, is that they are often informative without being compelling, a fact all too apparent in a book that only fleetingly sparks into life. Nevertheless, Gross has certainly done his homework and has a great deal to tell about the evolution of the character. Thus we learn that a role neglected in Shakespeare's own time was eventually resurrected by a drunken Irish actor, Charles Macklin, the first to play the part as anything other than a comic pantomime villain. He was followed by another drunk, Edmund Kean, who, discarding the traditional red wig – shades of Judas – was said to have given such an electrifying performance as the Jew that Coleridge described it as 'like reading Shakespeare by flashes of lightning'. But the great innovator was still to come in the august shape of Henry Irving, the founder of that narcissistic and self-congratulatory thespian style, still flourishing today, in which the actor is considered more important than the play. His gimmick was to play Shylock (originally billed by Shakespeare, it should not be forgotten, as 'a man of extreame crueltie') as a sympathetic character, a being who, in the words of a critic of the day, 'united the soul of Savonarola, the bearing of Charles the First, with just a touch of Lord Beaconsfield that made for mystery'. It was an intepretation that so outraged Shaw that he wrote: 'There was no question then of a good Shylock or a bad Shylock; he was simply not Shylock at all: and when his own creation came into conflict with Shakespeare's, as it did openly in the Trial Scene, he simply played in flat contradiction of the lines, and positively acted Shakespeare off the stage'. How often, I wonder, might we have applied these strictures to our own preening actors as they sacrificed a great role to their own ego and profile?

It is noticeable that when we come to the Shylocks of our own time and Gross is no longer peddling other people's views, but is able to express opinions on productions he has seen, the book takes a decided lift. He is clearly impatient of the pretentious and many of his observations on the contemporary theatre are not only apt, but have a refreshingly mordant bite about them. This is nowhere better exemplified than in his comments on Jonathan Miller's staging of *The Merchant of Venice* at the National Theatre in 1970. This, let me remind those who have blotted it out of memory, was the production that starred Laurence Olivier complete with fluting cut-glass accent, had a late Victorian setting, and, among other travesties, omitted such inconvenient lines as 'I hate him for he is a Christian'. Indeed, it was in many ways such a bizarre enterprise that it is a bit disconcerting to find Gross describing it as the key production of the period. But the reason behind this strange choice is soon explained: 'This production established the principle that a director is free to do whatever he likes with the play — to bend it, twist it, advertise his boredom with it; to spice it up with anachronisms; to steam-roller the poetry; to hit the audience over the head with what ought to be subtle implications.'

There it is in a nutshell, what is largely wrong with the British theatre, and I imagine there will be quite a few playwrights, neither writing in decameters nor dead, who will bless him for saying it. But I am less optimistic about how many actors will take note of his equally eloquent and truthful tribute to one of the lesser sung Shylocks, David Suchet: 'A welcome reminder that there are still actors who see their job as trying to do justice to the text, rather than use it as a trampoline for self-display.' For many, it would be like asking a peacock to stop preening its feathers.

Poetry

JOHN FORTH

Doing What You Do

Collected Poems by Charles Causley
(Macmillan. £12.99)

This book is unlikely to remind you of
W. S. Gilbert's young man of St. Bees
who, when stung on the arm by a wasp,
said he was so glad that it wasn't a
hornet. Apart from its economical statement on expectation and rhyme, that
limerick offers a glimpse of what the
master might have attempted had he
taken more time off. You'd be far more
likely to recall Frost's utmost of
ambition, which was to lodge a few
poems where they'll be hard to shift, for
many here have that look about them.
We're invited to join in as a mark of
ordinary decent respect, and so we do,
for in songs loved by childrn of all ages
Causley has few equals.

His 'Nursery Rhyme' and 'Green
Man In The Garden' were among the
best to confront the gap between wisher
and wished in the most simple terms,
where the heart's desire remains un-
attainable until it's no longer desired.
It's in the more ambitious verse too ('At
The British War Cemetery' or 'At
Grantchester') and it's there in others
that refuse to be shifted. The traditional
critique of Causley tells of a poet
cunning and dextrous at giving edge to
formal styles, especially the ballad,
whilst appearing lost in baggier shirts.

This was true of the early work where
some prosy naval studies have not worn
well, and almost true of the 1951-75
Collected, where only a small section of
new work promised a new direction. It is
much less so now that he has filled out
on travels and developed more muscle
for the poems on family history. A
hundred have been added to the earlier
book for this 75th birthday edition.

The themes show innocence under
threat and the need for sympathy and
vulnerability in the face of personal and
public monstrosity. Threat can be anything from a school bully or an accident
to all-out war, the recent poems looking
more often at localised kinds of
arbitrariness. He seems to have been
born with a hunger for poetic opportunity. When aunt Gwen in 'Bridie
Wiles' wonders if 'it all' (doing what you
do) was down to her dropping him on
his head as a baby she simply gives him
another poem.

Causley's earliest work was written
during war-time naval service and published in 1951. War was the killing of
Christ and man's sacrifice Christ's, but
these poems carry his Liberal-Christian
vision comparitively lightly (he says he
prefers an empty church to one filled
with sermons). In the recent beautifully
prepared 'Sunday School Outing' one of
his new characters assures us:

They always say
He's fond of little children,
Says Liza, voice of granite.
Well, now's He's chance.

The 'Quite unrelenting / All-day rain'
that follows is a fitting Causley finish.
When, much earlier, Henry and

Elizabeth attended 'King's College Chapel' and sat 'in their white lawn sleeves, as cool as history', every kind of potential was within them, as it was for 'Keats at Teignmouth' who courted, without seeking after resolution, 'death the lover' as well as the nightingale. It's always Heaven *and* Hell awaiting us (see 'Charlotte Dymond & Grandmother') – and this later becomes a suspended, attainable here and now remarkable for its lack of melodrama. 'Eden Rock' ends it all with a view of his parents:

They beckon me from the other bank.
I hear them call, *See where the stream-path is!*
Crossing is not as hard as you might think.

I had not thought that it would be like this.

Causley has travelled more than literally since his early days, but an aspect of the work that still secures his place beyond the modern sway, apart from the rolling rhythms and thunderous rhymes, is the tendency to use metaphor as a flag instead of a sail. This happens with the silence and wall-building of 'Silent Jack' and in the comparison of poet to stone-cutter in 'Richard Bartlett', but it's there in the opening Keats poem too. And sometimes the broad brush and diction suitable for pace and expliciteness in the ballads is used elsewhere and the effect is less sure. 'Crystal' and 'iron' were popular adjectives and 'snow' was everywhere. Much stronger was the relatively understated 'Seasons in North Cornwall' with its explicit but integral metaphor:

My room is a bright glass cabin,
All Cornwall thunders at my door,
And the white ships of winter lie
In the sea-roads of the moor.

Explicitness of rhyme, too, needs to be an opportunity rather than a problem, and although Causley can and will sell you anything from berry/merry and city/pity to tree/sea, the mingling of ancient and modern usually enables him to escape with the silver:

Blithely O blithely the casual morning
Burned life away as the leaf on a tree,
Rolling the sun like a mad hoop beside me,
˙And down at the end of the alley, the sea.

This is 'Devonport', sung to 'The Streets of Laredo', telling why the sailor is never home from sea. Times are placed and felt strongly in the use of visual detail, as in the later, evocative 'Gudow' describing an East-West guard-post and the sonnet '1940', spoken by one of the men dressed 'In second-best':

Glassed in the space between two lives, we
                                    test
The anxious air: file third-class cases on
The rack: observe the engine shake out pure
Blots of black water from its belly. Learn
Our travel-warrants off by heart. Wait for
The land to move; the page of war to turn.

These last two came in or around *Secret Destinations* (1984), though unfortunately the individual volumes aren't identified. They prove that Causley is marvellous at local description honed into universal theme, and although his admirers may say the poems are deceptively complex (as if to justify their simplicity), he's surely at his best with the pure and simple expressed simply.

Then he can sing like Housman and play like W. H. Davies. He can be as punchy (though not as funny or disturbing) as Plomer. Larkin saw him as a fellow Leo the stars got wrong. His book should be administered to the young in small doses by all teachers because it is infinitely more humane and various than the official advice on offer. In fact it should be an answer to everyone's dream of a truly popular treasure and, for sheer bulk and gorgeous bounty, it ought to be a roaring success.

Music

MERVYN HORDER

'Tell me the truth about Ben'

Benjamin Britten – a Biography by Humphrey Carpenter (Faber. £20)

So our Ben, the eternal schoolboy, pops up as third target – after Auden (1981) and Pound (1988) – at the far end of the well-appointed Humphrey Carpenter shooting gallery. The mark of a Carpenter biography is an extra density in the weave, simply more stitches to the square inch of his tapestry than other practitioners can manage; it is possible that he would be actually less happy with a more remote subject where

speculation had sometimes to replace the dexterous organization of thick contemporary documentation. There are a few Aldeburgh and other names missing from his list of interviewees, and it is a misfortune that he started on his job just after the death of Britten's sister, Beth Welford, and has apparently not had access to the material she was preparing for the second volume of her *My Brother Benjamin*; but apart from a slight slackening in the account of Britten's American years, the pursuit of the quarry is unrelenting and the readability voltage astonishingly sustained across nearly 600 pages, with no less than 100 photographs to support the whole.

There are two publics for this book: one of musicians hungry for any background intimations, small or great, which will enrich their sensitivity to the clash of the notes in Britten's formidably large and *sui generis* output; another of 'general readers' curious about the ups and downs of a prominent contemporary homosexual musician. The first class will find the gallery of supporting characters from the music and opera worlds clearly and fairly floodlit – bossy Auden, Pears the egocentric, Joan Cross the wise, Imogen Holst the scatty, the downtrodden Eric Crozier, and Ben's longest-standing (and most understanding) friends John and Myfanwy Piper; but the musicology in the book aims no higher than intelligent programme-note level, so that it is not possible to rank the book with the other two giant British music biographies of the century, Mosco Carner's *Puccini* and Norman Del Mar's

Richard Strauss, both of which are on the solider, more conventional Life & Works principle. No attempt, for example, is made to address the salient question why Britten couldn't write, or at least never wrote, a swinging tune, and had to climax so many of his best choral works with hymn tunes not his own; not that he didn't make superb use of them, but it remained a disability of which he was himself aware.

There is a small bonus of anecdotes. I liked the account of a performance of *Lucretia* in Italy where the curtain, supposed to fall just before the rape, got stuck, leaving Tarquinius in full view on the stage very much at a loss; loud exhortations of 'Coraggio, coraggio!' reached him from the audience. There is also the Snape village girl for whom Britten bought a ticket to a CEMA concert, and who gave him her opinion of it afterwards: 'Oh, I didn't mind it at all!'

As to the sex – both the central Pears affair and Ben's lifelong feeling of 'being lost without the company of the young' – it is all here: who shared the master's bed, who appeared suddenly from the bathroom with a towel round his waist and who without the towel, which of the flirtees flirted back, the kisses, the sighs, the misunderstandings, the ultimate cold shoulder (which Britten turned to so many of his adult friends as well) and all the rest of it. The sum of all the little fellows' testimony to their inquisitor is 'and nothing happened'. In Mrs Piper's words 'he kept the rules'. While it is the biographer's duty to unearth and record such things, there is the danger that the bizarre nature of the disclosures and the hearsay may cause them to loom larger in the bright-eyed reader's idle mind than they ever did in Britten's fantastically hectic daily life. We are perhaps too used to the facile Freudian concept of sublimation. Ben was a lateish child, born when his father was 36 and his mother 41; the tremendous psychic drive which this particular genius managed to channel, against chronic health handicaps, into producing and performing his highly original music was surely a far deeper and more mysterious current than any mere sex urge.

Performances of Britten's music have greatly increased in number since his death (the same being true of both Delius and Vaughan Williams); and as Hemingway reminds us, 'A major art cannot ever be judged until the unimportant physical rottenness of whoever made it is well buried.' Is it reasonable to hope now that Britten's uniquely voiced products will transcend their inherent difficulties, achieve universality, and find him a place up on the same high shelf as the three great individualists among composers of Western music – Mozart, Chopin and Debussy? Only time can decide. Today it may be Bent Britten, Peter's Queers, the Twilight of the Sods etc, etc. Tomorrow Immortality?

ROGER CALDWELL

Rag Bag

Stravinsky by Robert Craft (Lime Tree. £20)

The character of Stravinsky has been so extensively presented to us through the writings of Robert Craft that there is the danger of our being unable to see him whole from any other perspective: no one is able to monopolize the music but Craft has gone a long way towards monopolizing the life. Few writers have been closer to their subjects, and it is precisely this which gives one pause for doubt. For, from 1948 onwards when Craft became integrated into the Stravinsky household, he appears, by his own account, to have acquired an ascendancy over the older man so as to exert a decisive influence on Stravinsky's creative development. Craft claims to have educated Stravinsky in the ways of Schoenbergian serialism and thus to be instrumental in his adoption of the twelve-tone system. In the present work Craft goes further and claims an essential advisory role in all of Stravinsky's works after 1953. But for this collaboration, it would appear, such late works as the *Requiem Canticles* and *The Flood* either would not have taken the form they did or would not have been composed at all.

The story of Craft's ascendancy over the older man is a curious one, and one that by its nature requires to be told by an impartial third party. The tale given by Craft is that he helped Stravinsky out of a creative impasse by directing him towards Schoenbergian serialism about which he was previously ignorant. It is possible to doubt, however, the seriousness of Stravinsky's creative bloc, given that there is little evidence of a lengthy hiatus in the continuing production of new works, or that a composer as protean and ingenious as Stravinsky would not have by his own devices have refound his path without the aid of the younger man. Whether it would have taken the direction it did is another matter; certainly, Stravinsky did not take up the twelve-tone system until its creator was safely dead. If it is pointless to speculate what sort of music Stravinsky would have written without the intervention of Craft, it is undeniable that his, as it were, stepping into the dead man's shoes helped prolong the vogue for serialism.

From the vantage-point of the present-day it is difficult to conceive of a period when the future of music was seen to reside in a single approved system. There was no school of Stravinsky, but there was very much a school of Schoenberg, and its exponents were ubiquitous. In Argentina Alberto Ginastera flirted with twelve-tone rows, but did not allow it too much to interfere with his naturally colourful and uninhibited style. More serious was the case in Norway of Hilding Rosenberg who abandoned his native musical manners to embark on a series of durchcomponiert twelve-tone string quartets little listened-to today. In England, among the young generation of serialists, Peter Maxwell Davies wrote an earnestly dodecaphonic Trumpet Sonata in which little of his unique musical imagination is to be found. When Stravinsky too joined the serialist bandwagon there were cries of treason from some quarters, shouts of joy from others that he had finally seen the light. In fact, though Stravinsky's later serial music is, by comparison with the major ballets, little-known, there must be many listeners who have innocently enjoyed *Agon,* say, without suspecting that there was anything suspicious going on. Indeed, Stravinsky's formalist predilections and his then unfashionable interest in medieval and renaissance music meant that the procedures of twelve-tone music were at least not inimical to him. Adorno's famous study of 1948, *The Philosophy of Modern Music,* which vilifies Stravinsky and exalts Schoenberg, nonetheless expresses misgivings about his hero's attempts to marry the essentially pointilliste techniques of serialism with classic large-scale form (historically dependent on tonality) in such late works as the Piano Concerto. Here Stravinsky stays truer to the best insights of Schoenberg than does Schoenberg himself, though Adorno never came to consider the matter afresh. Adorno, like Schoenberg, was a neighbour of Stravinsky's in California, one too he had no wish to acknowledge.

Craft's latest Stravinsky book is something of a rag-bag – some pieces, it appears, were especially written for the book, others are of unspecified provenance. Despite the title, there is a fair amount of often illuminating but frequently technical musical analysis together with some essays which will be of interest only to the most devoted Stravinskyan. Most people, I suspect, who read the book will come to it, as I have done, already having devoured the preceding volumes of Conversations and Diaries, and eager for any further revelations about this most fascinating of men. The main features of Craft's Stravinsky are already before us: we are familiar with the mordant wit, the egotism, the anal-retentive character of the man, the intense intellectual acquisitiveness, yet the new book is not without its surprises. Stravinsky is presented here more than he has been before as a family man, and it has to be said that the picture is an unattractive one. Craft says that in some respects Stravinsky possessed a logic where other people possess a psychology; the result, though fascinating to read about, must sometimes have made Stravinsky hard to live with and does not excuse a certain callousness which is not exactly unknown in men of genius. The behaviour of his predatory and unpleasant children, as detailed by Craft, is, however, in no way redeemed by any traces in them of their father's genius.

Craft has undoubtedly served Stravinsky well. Of Schoenberg, who shares with him musical dominance in the first half of the present century, and who is no less intriguing a man than Stravinsky himself, the only biographical writing of note is the almost comically pedestrian account by Professor Stuckenschmidt, abysmally translated into English by Humphrey Searle. Any future biographer of Stravinsky will have a hard job ahead of him, so much has Craft already Boswellized him. Indeed, just as many now read Boswell's Life of Johnson without having read a word of the great man himself, so it must be presumed there are readers of Craft who are ignorant of Stravinsky's music but fascinated by the man. If there is a danger in this of making Stravinsky a 'personality', one should neither underestimate the artistry with which Craft has delineated that personality nor the exemplary value of such personalities when they come in such potent form as that of Craft's Stravinsky. Craft, like Boswell, presents us with the man in all his engaging (and sometimes un-engaging) quidditas. If one remembers best the acerbic witticisms – his encapsulation of Rachmaninov as 'Six foot four of Russian gloom' or his lapidary response to Britten's music: 'Who needs it?' – it is not advisable to take too lightly his dedication of one of his works 'to God and the Boston Symphony Orchestra'. For Stravinsky was a deeply religious man, as the hieratic nature of many of his works suggests, and a believer in the Devil. The exact nature of his belief remains obscure, but Craft's discovery after Stravinsky's death of the disproportionate number of books in his library about the Dominicans reveals not one of the least surprising facets of this most surprising of men.

LONDON MAGAZINE
April/May
Chun-Chen Yeh
on Chinese Theatre

Cinema

CHARLES DRAZIN

Poor Humans

Jean Renoir: Projections of Paradise by Ronald Bergan (Bloomsbury. £25.00)

Jean Renoir wrote in his memoirs that he had spent his life trying to determine the extent of his father's influence upon him. He felt that even when he went out of his way to repudiate the great painter's precepts, he was none the less subconsciously fulfilling them. This harmony of outlook between father and son is striking, and emerges as a major theme in Ronald Bergan's biography.

After the First World War Jean began his working life in ceramics, as his father had done. He married his father's ex-model, Dedée Heuchling, and in 1924, five years after Auguste's death, would become a film-maker, by his own account to make her a star. Just as Auguste had painted Dedée, so Jean would film her. The early years were full of setbacks, and soon Jean parted company with both his wife and several of his father's paintings, sold to finance his films. However, he compensated for the loss of the paintings by continuing his father's work in another medium. Films such as *La Partie de campagne* or *Boudu sauvé des eaux* put the joie de vivre of Auguste's paintings into motion. Jean would write in his memoirs of Auguste's belief in the 'oneness of the world' and 'a love of all living things'. And it is this sympathy that is the essence of Renoir's films and which, in the words of François Truffaut, 'succeeded in creating the most alive films in the history of the cinema'.

Renoir was not given to making moral pronouncements but effectively articulated his standpoint in the prologue of puppets that opened his first major sound film, *La Chienne*. Guignol declares that the audience are about to see a work that is neither a drama nor a comedy, and in which the characters are neither heroes nor villains, but just 'poor humans like you and me'. Renoir regarded creating drama as secondary to reproducing the rhythm of life. Of *Toni* he wrote, 'I attached as much importance to the countrywoman surprised while doing her washing as to the hero of the story . . . My aim was to give the impression that I was carrying a camera and microphone in my pocket and recording whatever came my way, regardless of its comparative importance.'

Such an attitude would earn a cuff round the ear in a Hollywood scriptwriting class, so it was hardly surprising that when Renoir arrived in America in 1940 he would suffer severe culture shock. Engaged by Twentieth Century-Fox to make a film set in the Georgia swamps, he naively assumed that he and the crew would go off to Georgia. The studio executives had to explain to him that the swamps would be recreated in Hollywood. They hadn't spent millions building a studio, where they could simulate anything, to have upstart foreigners shooting on location.

Renoir would soon come to feel that effectively his only role in the film was to say 'Action' and 'Cut'. Any scene that displeased the studio boss Daryl Zanuck would be reshot. Zanuck concluded that 'Renoir has a lot of talent, but he's not one of us', and Renoir's contract was terminated by mutual agreement. He was to find that Twentieth Century-Fox was fairly typical of Hollywood as a whole. In the years that followed suitable projects were hard to come by, although when he was permitted the artistic freedom he was used to in France, he produced fine work. *The Southerner* is true to his principles and stands comparison with the best of his French films.

Jean Renoir's views on his experience of Hollywood were characteristically generous. In spite of his unhappy time at Twentieth Century-Fox he wrote that 'Zanuck is a genius in his own way. He has contrived, while using industrial methods, to give his work the undeniable stamp of quality.' Renoir's quarrel was with the system itself. He conceived of himself as a craftsman, not a functionary in a process of mass production. 'My dream,' he wrote, 'is of a craftsman's cinema in which an author can express himself as directly as the painter in his paintings or the writer in his books.' Nothing could have seemed more natural to Auguste Renoir's son, but America was the last place on earth in which to resist the machine-dominated tide of modern progress. Europe beckoned.

In 1955 he made *French Cancan,* his first film in France for sixteen years. It marked a triumphant return to his roots.

The screen becomes a window on the Montmartre of his childhood, its streets miraculously brought to life. The film radiates the joy of someone greeting a long-lost friend and one senses Renoir's relief to be back on home ground. But these years would be as notable for the films he inspired as those he made. When a new generation of would-be directors looked to him for guidance, he was accessible and enthusiastic. Louis Malle describes him as 'the father of the New Wave', and it is hard to imagine how that revolution could have taken place without him. The lyricism of the work of film-makers such as Truffaut, Rohmer or Malle, the priority they accorded to the inconsequential eddies of life, were a reaffirmation of Renoir's humanist vision.

Ronald Bergan has performed the admirable feat in his biography of not only distilling the spirit of Renoir but also writing with that spirit: he sets about his task with the sympathy and love that his subject showed in his films. But his obvious admiration does not blind him: he neither idealizes Renoir nor refrains from pointing out the inconsistencies in his behaviour. When he deals with the films, his comments are succinct and apposite. He usefully includes several of Renoir's synopses and ideas for films that were never made. They show how consistently productive Renoir's mind was, even into his old age. So much has been previously written about Renoir that inevitably Bergan recycles a lot of old material, but he also assembles a substantial collection of extremely illuminating first-hand sources. The friends and family of Renoir had sufficient trust in Bergan to confide their memories and their participation lends the work extra authority. This is certainly a book for devotees of Renoir, but also for those who share his vision of a craftsman's cinema in an age when Hollywood is as dominant as ever.

Selected Books

IAN JEFFREY

Brain Incarnate

Michel Foucault. By Didier Eribon. Translated by Betsy Wing (Faber. £25)

A life of Foucault! In his *Archaeology of Knowledge* (1969) he offered a kind of warning: 'Do not ask who I am and do not ask me to remain the same: leave it to our bureaucrats and our police to see that our papers are in order'. Neither that injunction nor Foucault's own antipathy to subjectivism seems to have deterred Didier Eribon, presently working as an editor with *Le Nouvel Observateur*.

What exactly is Eribon's book? Ostensibly, it is a biography, justified by Foucault's fame as a philosopher. As a philosopher? Well, perhaps as a historian. Historians, though, might object. Here, for instance, is a brief extract from Mark Poster's *Foucault, Marxism & History* (1984) – and Poster is by no means unsympathetic: 'The writing is thick and metaphoric and the point of view of the narrative line is often lost. The object of investigation is never quite clarified and appears to be neither individuals, nor groups, nor institutions. What is worse, things seem to shift in the course of the writing; at the beginning one issue is at stake, by the end we seem to be reading about something else'. In that rather lucid book Poster went on to give an account of Foucault's seemingly eccentric procedures. In a biography you might expect to find the writer's thought evaluated, and its principal shifts noted and explained. Why otherwise take an interest in his life? Eribon, however, appears to have no more than a cursory interest in his subject's intellectual trajectory.

Why, in fact, bother to write the life of someone who spent most of his waking hours in the Bibliothèque Nationale taking notes in a neat hand? Because in 1984 after, and probably because of, a visit to California he died of Aids, at a time when the disease was still something of a legend. The book ends with a doctor's statement published in *Le Monde* on his septicemic condition at the end. That is to say: the most celebrated intellectual of the 1970s, author of one contentious and successful text after another, is brought low by California, epicentre of the new hedonism.

'Cerebral suppuration': the doctors' text is unsparing. At the same time the biography makes something of a play on Foucault's total baldness, via a picture by Martine Franck of Magnum. The philosopher-historian looked, and seemingly meant to look, like a hybrid fungus/phallus – a point which is picked up by the illustrator Adrian George in *The Times*'s review of Eribon's book (August 13th). The Foucault who projected himself as the brain incarnate was also a connoisseur of grim endings. The most famous passage in his many volumes occurs at the beginning of *Discipline and Punish* (or *Surveiller et Punir*) of 1975, and it concerns the death on 2 March 1757 of the regicide Damiens, as quoted in the *Gazette d'Amsterdam*. Damiens was killed elaborately and publicly in the Place de Grève by what sound like trialists for a Carry On film on that theme. He was meant at the last to be torn limb from limb, but the horses on hand for the job weren't up to it, and after delays had to be supplemented. Although glossed by subsequent commentators and declared serious in intent, the Damiens episode represents something like a revenge of the contingent, and stands in the same teasing and transgressive revelation to the book as that blatantly naked and upright scalp stands to the institutionally engrossed life of the philosopher.

Eribon's book may be of little use to anyone interested in the shifts in Foucault's thought, but it is extraordinarily forthcoming on daily life in the academic and intellectual circles in which he moved. For anyone who ever wondered if the French intelligentsia is constituted of permanent scholarship boys there is food for thought here, in a text which charts any amount of manoeuvering and manipulating for the sake of plum jobs. *Michel Foucault* reads at times like a socialite's register of those in attendance at lectures and on interview panels, and the hero's disappointment at filling minor placings in national examinations is palpable. It is not exactly a demystifying treatment which explains everything in terms of peer group competitiveness, but it does leave some ground for thinking that the whole career amounted to a game, albeit oppressively intense. Why, for instance, should he gave been so keen on getting to the top of the tree, which was an election to the Collège de France in 1970? It looks as if he wanted security and recognition above all, even if afterwards he did go ostentatiously radical. The books suggests, even if it doesn't say so in so many words, that the radicalism of the 1970s was somehow part of a career structure which would establish him as an intellectual on the national stage, as a successor to Sartre. The radicalism of the '70s involved action on behalf of Solidarity in Poland, and for prison reform in France. He intervened, to his credit, over death sentences in Franco's Spain, and was, for a time, an enthusiast for Khomeini's Iran. He was, by Eribon's reckoning, a tireless and effective worker for good causes, but there is always something tantalising with respect to his motivation. Was he sincere? That, though, is an English question, out of keeping in relation to an activist for whom the truth lay in the acting.

The weakness of Eribon's book is that it takes Foucault's importance for granted. Apropos of *Les Mots et les Choses,* his first great success – in 1966 – Sartre said that it was somehow expected, a book designed for that particular time. The later books on incarceration and sexuality, seem to have been unusually apposite, and to have caught the contemporary imagination. Although Eribon's list of influential teachers and colleagues are unfailingly interesting they throw no light on that major question. Nor are there many motifs or vignettes sharp enough to be suggestive. Foucault hardly appears in anything like spontaneous action, except for one impetuous journey in his Jaguar from Uppsala, where he was a cultural officer, to Paris for the May events of 1958. That little story, though, ends with no more than a whimper. Then for most of the turbulent 1960s he was out of the country. Eribon, cautious and respectful throughout, seems to suggest that in 1968-69, when Foucault was head of the philosophy department at Vincennes, he may have had a kind of awakening even if the results only began to show later. Perhaps his appointment to the Collège de France finally gave him the security he needed to live his life, or whatever parts of it had escaped him in the Bibliothèque Nationale.

JEREMY LEWIS

Scavenging

Stephen Spender: A Portrait with Background by Hugh David (Heinemann. £17.50)

Early on in their friendship, Stephen Spender asked W. H. Auden – in a 'choking moment of hope mingled with despair' – whether his poetry was really any good. Of course it was, Auden replied, 'because you are so infinitely capable of being humiliated. Art is born of humiliation.' Spender has, over the years, attracted more than his share of hostility and ridicule, most memorably at the hands of Evelyn Waugh, yet one of his most engaging qualities has been his readiness to admit and to examine his own failings and inconsistencies, whether social, sexual, literary or political. A tirelessly autobiographical writer, he shares with his friend Cyril Connolly an almost masochistic fascination with his own shortcomings, disarming in advance whose who look askance at his combination of innocence and ambition, his sexual ambivalence, and his espousal of left-wing politics while simultaneously relishing country house life, high society and (in Hugh David's words) 'toddling out to dinner parties' with the grand and influential.

All this is spelled out, admirably and in adequate detail, in Spender's autobiography, *World Within World,* which was published in 1951 and takes us up to the end of the War. Hugh David's study of the poet covers the same ground as the earlier book, so much so that the last forty years of his subject's life are dealt with in half as many pages; but since Spender has – not unreasonably, as it turns out – refused permission for his own writings to be quoted, his biographer has had to reply more than might otherwise have been the case on the published works of (for example) Christopher Isherwood and T. C. Worsley, and on paraphrases of Spender's own words, slanted in such a way as to portray him in as unflattering

and demeaning a light as possible. For example, when describing the party that followed his wedding to Inez Pearn, Spender tells us of how

Among the wedding presents were a few toast racks, silver trays and so forth. Seized with a sudden impulse of pity for those amongst my friends who were paupers, I thrust these upon them as they left. In the middle of the wedding party, a special messenger arrived with proofs of a magazine article for me to correct. I went into a room alone and looked over these, not without a sense of self-importance . . .

David's version reads: 'Ostentatiously, Spender withdrew from the festivities in order to correct some proofs and then returned to demonstrate his new political sympathies by distributing the wedding presents among his "pauper" friends.'

But all this lies in the future, for David starts out with Spender's literary grandmother, who – we are told twice on the first page – died in 1895, had a Spanish mother (several pages later she has become an Italian) and lived after her marriage in Bath, where 'the explorer David Livingstone was a near (but presumably absent) neighbour until his death in Old Chitambo in what was then Northern Rhodesia in 1873' (as proves so often the case, this is inaccurate as well as irrelevant, since Rhodesia wasn't named as such until 1895).

Such peccadilloes are harmless enough, if indicative of a somewhat casual approach to the facts: but once Spender himself steps into the author's sights, David's approach combines the leering and the tendentious with the kind of gush one associates with an old-fashioned romantic novel. 'He still loved his father,' David tells us of Spender as a child in Norfolk during the First World War: 'But he loved his mother too. Surely *she* wasn't a Hun or a Jerry . . . Or was she? Why did she shout at him? And why she now so often ill, in bed at home or away in hospitals and nursing homes? *It hadn't always been like this.* Once, once . . .' Spender's poem 'My Parents', in which he describes the reaction – half-fearful, half-attracted – of a sheltered, timid, upper middle-class child to the local village boys, is produced as evidence of an incipient and long-lasting fascination with 'rough trade'. Nor is Spender's childhood interest in butterflies immune from his biographer's prurient gaze: Spender tells us of how 'Sometimes, stuck as though glued to the stem of a flower, just below the cup of the petals, there was a chalk blue butterfly . . . In the sun the butterflies expanded and then shut close their wings with the exact movement of a hinge. When the hinge was shut the closed wings were of a knife-blade thickness, so that you could not have split them with the edge of a razor' – which is paraphrased by Hugh David as 'There were butterflies fumbling the hollyhocks in the garden, or waiting in a concupiscent torpor, their wings so tightly folded that a razor blade would not prise them apart.'

Spender's time at Oxford includes a stale and irrelevant evocation of the Brideshead world and a by now familiar flurry of solecisms, including undergraduates catching the last train back from Euston (twice), Christ Church college, and Rosamond Lehmann as a fellow-student (in fact she was at Cambridge; he also misspells her first name). David affects at times a manly, joshing manner of speech, unafraid of referring to the 'intellectual gravy train' or the 'bottom-pinching amorality of Bloomsbury', and summarising the poetic ambitions of Auden and his acolytes with Blytonesque breeziness ('What fun they all had plotting and scheming and aesthetic *putsch*!'): he tells us, apropos Spender's infatuation with a fellow-undergraduate, that 'once again he had made what was plainly a pitch for physical experience, only to limp wounded and disappointed from the field,' but it was in the Hamburg of rent-boys and male prostitues that – according to this lubricious version of events – he really came into his own ('This was it! This was the Germany Spender had been looking for!').

David affects a bluff familiarity with the literary world ('Good old Tom!' he remarks after informing us that T. S. Eliot had written the blurb for a volume of Spender's poems), but he shows no interest whatsoever in Spender as a writer; indeed, since he so evidently dislikes and despises his subject, one wonders why he has chosen to write about him at all, let alone during his lifetime. He refers gleefully to 'hack work' and 'pot-boiling' done for 'quick money', and suggests that Spender's short-lived and informal role as co-editor of *Horizon* 'did more for his reputation than any number of privately printed pamphlets, any amount of self-absorbed scribbling': he then goes on to suggest that Cyril Connolly founded *Horizon* to escape the world of Woolton Pies (which had yet to be invented), misleadingly quotes 'Palinurus' – published in 1944 – in such a way as to suggest he was writing in 1939, and tells us that Spender 'insouciently (*sic*) lunched at the Café Royal' with Geoffrey Grigson in October that same year. Quite why the lunch – unlike David's spelling –should be described as 'insouciant' is not made clear (in fact Grigson was giving advice on the setting up of *Horizon,* something the author forgets to tell us in his anxiety to portray Spender as a social-climbing butterfly): but long words are hardly Hugh David's *forte* –elsewhere he has difficulties with 'numinous', as well as giving us 'dependant' and 'Lucien' Freud.

This shoddy and repellant little book reflects badly only on its author and its publisher (who has been quoted as blithely remarking that any errors can always be corrected in a reprint): even so, I shudder to think who will be the next victim of this literary scavenger.

C. J. FOX

Death-Masks

Keepers of the Flame by Ian Hamilton (Hutchinson. £18.99)

Ian Hamilton's new book, sub-titled 'Literary Estates and the Rise of Biography', comes at an apt time, since we now live in an Age of Biography. For instance, this reviewer recently approached one of the great combines now in control of British publishing with a proposal for a collection of literary essays by Richard Aldington, most of whose critical output – vivid and blazingly independent – has been buried for decades in the catacombs of the Colindale Newspaper Library. The idea was received with a shrug and the ingenuous proposer was told that a biography highlighting Aldington's amorous adventures between the wars might stand a chance of acceptance, but not anything he'd written. One of the combine's member firms – formerly a prestigious House, now a mere nameplate – used to publish Aldington, so there was no special grudge against his work. Rather, I was informed, this was a time when biographies were the thing and the actual writings of such figures from the past had little market appeal.

Voices raised against this state of affairs are few indeed. C. H. Sisson's is one of them. He has questioned the whole basis of biographies claiming to capture the 'truth' about, in particular, writers of the Nineteenth and Twentieth centuries, with the surfeit of documentation afforded by these epochs. After all, said Sisson, the subject of a literary biography is a specialist in words and, if he is a poet, they are his very *raison d'être.* 'In what sense can the biographer be said to get at a truth which the subject's words have not revealed?' Granted, there are facts of birth, death, friends and abodes to be presented. But, asked Sisson, what can an assemblage of such facts ultimately amount to except another memorial to set beside the subject's works? Kathleen Jones, in a new biography of Christina Rossetti, had conceded that 'finding' Christina was not easy. To which Sisson, writing in the *P. N. Review,* riposted: 'The best – the only – place to look for her is in her works; the most that can be claimed for the "finder" is that she tells us something about the outer circumstances in which the work was produced.'

This is, at the very least, a good corrective to the assumptions which, along with market considerations, underlie the storm of tittle-tattle unleashed of late by successive Lives of eminent pen-persons. For its part, Hamilton's book deals with the efforts, sometimes bizarre, made through the literary estates of star authors, from Donne to Larkin, to manage their 'after-fame', the Keepers of Flame pursuing their posthumous image-moulding mainly through the agency of authorised biography. But in recounting the widely varying results of these efforts, Hamilton doesn't challenge the prevalence of gossip over literature, now or at times in the past, which follows from the primacy of the biographical. Thus he plays down the implications of the resounding comment he quotes from Wordsworth decrying the emphasis on Robert Burns as philandering toper in Currie's Life of the poet. Rather like Sisson, Wordsworth maintained that if the works of a poet were good, they contained within themselves all that was necessary for comprehension and relish. 'The least weighty objection to heterogeneous details, is that they are mainly superfluous, and therefore an encumbrance.'

The world, however, would have its

'heterogeneous details' and *Keepers of the Flame* is, apart from occasional lapses into an odd species of stylistic flipness, an engaging account of the methods, ranging from wholesale destruction of letters to doctoring of records, by which such posthumous curiousity is met or fended off. It is not until he reaches Dryden that Hamilton really gets to grips with his subject. We are shown how Dryden's ghost thrived through the machinations of his dedicated publisher Tonson, just as the dead Pope left behind a fanatical booster in the person of Warburton.

With Johnson, the book becomes an analysis of how the Doctor came to be seen after his demise in a way imagined by Boswell. Edmund Wilson effectively sorted out that situation fifty years ago. 'It is a pity,' Wilson wrote, 'that Boswell's *Life of Johnson* should so largely have supplanted for the general reader the writings of Johnson himself.' Wilson's exercise in de-Boswellisation, however, is not mentioned here. But Hamilton does provide an absorbing narrative of the ultimate discovery of the Boswell treasures at Fettercairn in 1930. In the preceding century, given the anxieties of the Eminent and their executors about unsavoury revelations, the story was often one of excision and incineration. 'The would-be biographer in those days,' says Hamilton of the Victorian time, 'worked to the sound of snipping scissors and paper crackling in the grate.'

His chapter on Carlyle centres on the row over the disclosures made about the Sage of Craigenputtock by Froude in what Hamilton calls 'the most heartfelt and compelling of Victorian biographies'. Froude emerges from Hamilton's pages as something of a hero and it is perhaps symptomatic of a weakness for literary biographies as against the primacy of their subjects' work that the evaluation here of the Froude portrait contrasts with the one offered in Julian Symons's 1952 book on Carlyle. According to Symons, the Froude biography was 'brilliant but over-dramatic'. It had helped 'to shift interest from the work to the man, and to create a picture, which has only a limited truth, of a half-mad figure with some unpleasant racial theories, whose genius lay chiefly in making other people unhappy'.

Hamilton details the lengths to which mothers, and of course, widows have gone in seeing to the construction of what W. E. Henley, in slating the semi-official biography of R. L. Stevenson, referred to as the 'barley-sugar effigy of a real man'. Yet even the most cunningly concocted barley sugar crumbles after a time, especially now that so many freebooting biographers roam the scene in search of effigies to debunk. This iconoclastic spirit Hamilton traces back to Lytton Strachey. Alas, the author of *Eminent Victorians* has himself fallen victim to retrospective ridicule – 'the Old Maid, not less funny because of the long and pastiche-looking beard . . . this extremely tall perverse amorist' – though Hamilton doesn't note this ironic twist of events.

Still, his section on Larkin prepares us for the blizzard of small-talk already blowing up with the publication of the poet's letters. On the other hand, militant feminists will bristle at his obvious sympathy for Ted Hughes over the Plath saga. Elsewhere, he doesn't bother to explain, either in his text or in his random footnotes, why he regards Aldington the biographer as belonging 'unappealingly' to the Strachey school of denigration when most of Aldington's books in the genre – the lives of Voltaire, Wellington, D. H. Lawrence, Mistral and (decidely unofficial) Stevenson – are in fact laudatory. Aldington's pioneering debunk of T. E. Lawrence, which presumably is the book Hamilton is thinking of at this point, merely fulfils a dictum of its author acceptable, surely, to Hamilton: 'The principle that you aren't to say anything impolite about the work or character of a writer who has been dead twenty years destroys both honest criticism and honest biography. Why must we be so damned mealy-mouthed?'

DIGBY DURRANT

Seekers

Loneliness and Time: British Travel Writing in the Twentieth Century by Mark Cocker (Secker and Warburg. £18.50)

It is hard to imagine a man, after a day scaling the terrible peaks of Tibet, would be so indifferent to the leeches that had settled on him that he stood, 'with blood oozing out of his boots as oblivious as a small child whose face is smeared with jam'. Frederick ('Eric')

Bailey, who noted this characteristic indifference of his assistant, Captain Morshead, was, like him, a meticulous and hardy geographer. An unimaginative man, his story of another expedition that involved his dressing up as Serbian officer and pasting on false badges with apricot preserve was accepted as readily as the account he gave of being hired by the Russians to track himself down as dangerous British spy. Life was always dangerous for Bailey, though not always in this comic opera way. So it was for Burton and Speke searching for the source of the Nile and for Philby, father of Kim, who was to claim that 650,000 square kilometres of unmapped desert, including the waterless tract of Rub-al-Khali, the Empty Quarter, had been 'dissected, belabelled and described' by him.

Why did they do it? Mark Cocker takes the conventional view that Britain's unexciting climate and landscape, tightness of morals and rigidity of class, once bred heroic misfits, particularly from amongst those whose relationships with their fathers had been unsympathetic. Before 1914 Britain needed these free spirits to take the unnecessary risks needed to defend and enlarge the Empire. Morshead was covered in leeches because he was part of the team mapping Tibet so that the Raj would be better informed to protect itself from the hordes of Russians who, it was feared by those who played the Great Game, might one day swoop into Tibet and on to the plains of India.

Earlier Speke and Burton had ignored the Blue Nile – which was more important than the White, providing six-sevenths of the river's flow – because its source was known and lay in the hands of Ethiopia while that of the White was unknown and led explorers into parts of Egypt, Kenya and the Sudan that would eventually become part of the Empire.

Similar personalities, born later in the Twenties and Thirties, would no doubt have submerged their private conflicts in equally patriotic ways, but the resources of the Empire no longer ran to such extravagance, and they were obliged to do without the benefits of its camouflage. Thesiger went to Arabia to find tribes living primitive lives as old as those of the Abyssinians in whose country he'd spent the first nine years of his childhood. Gavin Maxwell joined him a while, seeking another outlet for his tormented restlessness, and van der Post, rather like Thesiger, went into the bush of South Africa in search of ancient tribal customs.

Patrick Leigh Fermor went for a long walk across Europe when still a youth and never in any real sense returned; nor did Lawrence Durrell, who set off from Bournemouth in search of sex, which became less compelling ('saturated and exhausted, bored to death with sex'), but remained in a state of permanent enchantment.

Travel writers who are admired for their refusal to settle for the humdrum do not necessarily make good writers, though there is a conspiracy to pretend that the uncomfortable and often dangerous experiences they describe confer on them a talent that in truth they sometimes lack.

There's no need for any of that here. With the exception of Bailey and Philby, all of Cocker's travellers are acclaimed writers. They observe as closely as the two cartographers, but instead of boiling thermometers at the summits of mountains to calculate their height it is the 'off-moments of psychological significance' they choose to chart. This makes them more like novelists than *bona fide* travellers in many people's eyes and Durrell, Fermor, and van der Post in particular, with their flights of fancy, their over-stylishness, their love of words, deepen this suspicion – which is unlikely to be allayed by discovering that Fermor from early childhood was addicted to saying things backwards.

It is understandable that Cocker should be overawed by the company he's chosen to keep and this shows itself in his occasional lapses into a stiff and self-concious style that makes the going hard; but the absorbing detail makes his book an excellent companion to Fussell's *Abroad*.

DENIS HILLS

Estranged Exile

African Laughter: Four Visits to Zimbabwe by Doris Lessing (Harper/Collins. £16.99)

Doris Lessing, twice married and divorced (her second husband was a German Communist), arrived in England from Southern Rhodesia in 1949, bringing with her the manuscript of her first novel, *The Grass is Singing,* and her youngest child. Her Communist sympathies – she joined the Communist Party in 1949 – had upset the white Rhodesian establishment; and as *persona non grata,* though she had left the Communist Party in 1956, she was to remain in exile for over thirty years until in the 1980s she made several revisits to what had now become Zimbabwe. The resulting collection of African impressions is in part nostalgic and lyrical, in part a cautionary tale showing the author's disillusionment at the way things have turned out in black Zimbabwe. We are told how, after a happy childhood at the family farm in Lomagundi, she became resentful of settler life, its boredom, self-indulgence, sterotypes and racial prejudice – all of which she cruelly exposed in her anti-white satire *The Grass is Singing*. The book under review ends with the chastened reflections of an estranged exile weighing up the death of a colony and the disappointing consequences of black rule.

Doris Lessing's childhood idyll is symbolised by her love of camping out at night in the bush with her family – 'lying out with no roof between me and the sky was a gift not to be wasted . . . And I fell asleep and woke with the sun on my face, not the moon, my brother curled like a cat, my mother already at work folding up the bedding, and perhaps the "boy" asleep, his back to us.' Her subsequent revolt against white Rhodesian values was to destroy the idyll. Looking back now on this phase of alienation, she sees herself as something of a 'prig' and an 'idiot', distributing Communist propaganda in a Salisbury suburb and preaching revolution as a cure for everything.

By the time Doris Lessing revisited Southern Rhodesia (now Zimbabwe) in 1982 the terrorist war was over and great changes were taking place. A new black elite had seized power. The remaining white population, still in a state of shock, was bewailing the fate of Rhodes's paradise ('We had the best country and the best blacks in Africa,' Smith used to say). Mismanagement and corruption were rampant, Mugabe's senior officials drove about in a cavalcade and had built themselves palaces, and squatters were ravaging the countryside. Doris Lessing was especially pained by land erosion, 'the emptying and thinning of the bush, how the animals had gone,and the birds and insects, and this meant that everything had changed.' These changes, she writes, were 'more important than even the War, or the overthrow of the whites, the coming of the black government'. Squatters were planting mealies everywhere, denuding the soil, deepening the gullies, burning and felling trees. All the whites could do was to curse on their verandahs 'in the nagging peevish voices of spoiled children' (one recalls the 'high vexed colonial voices' of local whites which Graham Greene had overheard in the Belgian Congo).

Doris Lessing had a poignant reconciliation with her brother at his farm near Marandellas. Despite their divergent experiences – her brother had served in the Navy in World War Two and later took part in patrols against Mugabe's terrorists – they were able to discuss amicably their differences. Lessing also visited the forested highlands of the Vumba. It grieved her to see how crude cultivation was now despoiling them. Owing to its exposed position on the Mozambique frontier, the Vumba salient had been one of the most dangerous places to live in during the terrorist war, with armed bands constantly infiltrating it to stab, burn and shoot white families, missionaries, teachers and the farmer's labour force (native headmen might be flayed alive as sell-outs). At the height of the raids the present reviewer was staying with a white farmer who lived in a wired stockade in the Vumba. Doris Lessing's son, John Wisdom, was a neighbour and my host took me to see him – but don't mention Lessing's name, he warned me, 'she's a Commie'. Sitting among the honeysuckle on Wisdom's *stoep* discussing the war and his fear of a Russian invasion, three ageing white men in crumpled shorts and floppy hats, with our FN rifles propped against a wall, we must have looked like throwbacks to a colonial past.

The oddest people, in fact, had congregated in this remote green corner of Africa: single ladies with fierce dogs, cane-drinkers, retired majors from India, Scottish hoteliers, anglers and coffee-planters. There was something almost Wodehousian in such a society. They lived under daily threat of bullets and land mines. They were in debt to their bank managers. Their labour force was deserting. They chugged about in mine-proofed Land Rovers, sat in their lounges by lamp-light with a gun on the table, went early to bed with their anxieties to await the safety of dawn, when the first bulbul song would signal the allclear for another day. Doris Lessing missed all this, which is a pity, for she would have found much to admire in the courage, though not wrongheadedness, of her bigoted old compatriots, and she might now think better of them and of their achievements. Ironically, when she managed to revisit her parents' old homestead, she found it had become a squatters' slum of broken buildings, burned bush and trees, and unfriendly children. The idyllic scene of her youth, on which years before she had turned her back, had vanished. She stood there almost in tears.

The most satisfactory part of Doris Lessing's 1988 visit was her work with a team of African women (the Book Team) setting up an adult education project for villagers. At discussion groups she learned to appreciate the good humour and sound sense of simple Africans and the roots of their conservatism. At one meeting the male chairman told his audience, 'If you want to know why your husbands take new women then you have only to look at your wedding photographs.' It was generally agreed that 'freedom for women is for outside the home, but inside the old ways are the best.' The book's later chapters include a lengthy analysis of current problems in liberated Zimbabwe. Like Nadine Gordimer, Doris Lessing is a formidable critic of the white man's controversial role in Southern Africa. But she tends to sermonise, and goes on and on with her grim story. Yet the title of her book is *African Laughter*.

MARTIN ELLIOTT

Infantilism, Incest, Insects

Fraud by Anita Brookner (Cape. £14.99)
Angels and Insects by A. S. Byatt (Chatto & Windus. £14.99)

I wrote, in LM a year ago, that Anita Brookner was an elegant spectator and speculator at the window, and that the 1991 version of her annual novel (*A Closed Eye*) was particularly strong on the window motif: her heroine, throughout that book, had several glazed periods of yearning and regretting but certainly never broke the glass. The latest Brookner, *Fraud*, has two heroines, and one of these actually varies the metaphor, going so far as to retreat from the window in order to turn off the light and sit in the dark. This, yet again, is an apt motif for the Brookner-Woman who, notoriously by now, is dim about that thing outside called life. (The memorable Kitty Maule for example, in *Providence* (1982), quite simply lacked essential information which everyone else possessed but which she had somehow missed.) Brookner has spun yet another yarn about life as lived, or unlived, by South Kensingtonian-type women, who are typically widowed, or unmarried, and who are disturbed in their essentially maidenly centres by predatory, rather magnetic men, as well as by the more vulgar women who have gone easily to the market place knowing their price. The repetition of these types puts one in mind of Jane Austen, for Brookner has a little bit of ivory, which she works obsessively, and which is probably even more restricted than Austen's; while Brookner also has something of the stylishness which Austen had (Austen had other things as well, of course, notably a sense of fun, and a relish for individual character inside the type). The consummate use of consonance and assonance in 'It is a truth universally acknowledged, that a single man in possession of a good fortune must be in want of a wife' (opening of *Pride and Prejudice*) has some parallel in 'The facts, as far as they could be ascertained, were as follows' – with which Brookner begins *Fraud*. And throughout *Fraud* it is the decorous bravura of the language that holds you, making you read on to the end despite the lack of story and despite the sterile sad quality of the unheroic lives. Anna knows that she is 'uncomfortable to be with, had little to offer but her maidenly accomplishments and her letter writing and her too careful clothes.' Precisely.

What distinguishes this book from its eleven annual predecessors is its formal definition of the central problem of infantilism – the condition that affects fifty year old children, those polite, dutiful people who live-in with their elderly parents and who resolutely do not, cannot, grow up. Anna, on the death of her mother, turns to another elderly lady, Mrs Marsh, whom she persistently calls 'Aunt Vera' despite her lack of family connection and despite

Vera Marsh's reluctance to 'adopt' this embarrassing retard – harsh word 'retard', but that is what Brookner's heroines so often emotionally are.

This does not stop Brookner from being, probably, our most accomplished spinner of yarns (once called spinsters) in the classical-romantic Austenish tradition. It is still a pleasure to have central characters who can think in terms of the French poets – *Mes ancêtres, dans des appartements solonnels, tous idiots ou maniaques* – and who visit the Ingres in the Louvre for what they tell us of satisfaction in the real world. If Dr Brookner could, for one year at least, take leave from her task of reclaiming for the cast of modern fiction those lonely, or elderly, souls whom no-one but God would otherwise appreciate, and give us another factual account of the French painting on which she is, or was, a professional expert, I for one would be delighted. Or, alternatively, if she would write us a mystery story, what an addition she might make to that genre – the opening chapter of *Fraud* has some terse, Simenon-like dialogue, while the Brookner police inspector who finds a female octogenerian reliable as a witness on the basis of her pedantically correct use of *whom* is a welcome first cousin of Tey's Inspector Grant . . .

After *Possession*, A. S. Byatt continues to reconstruct the 19th century with *Angels and Insects,* two intricated novellas, in which she considers first the century's great science-versus-religion matter and then the lesser but linked topic of spiritualism. Byatt is less of a stylist than Brookner, but uses modes of writing more – the dialogue is consciously on stilts – so that she can be included in that growing breed of novelists who, so to speak, parody a previous writing style not for Joycean purposes of fun and appositeness but rather out of solemn imitation. Amongst such writers are William Golding (for his *Rites of Passage* trilogy), Peter Ackroyd (for *Hawksmoor* etc). It is not a total fashion to write thus – other writers still address the past using current diction and syntax (see, for example, Judith Chernaik's recently fluent *Mab's Daughters* on the Shelley women). But it is a distinct kind of historical work that one mustn't call historical fiction in the accepted sense. Moreover, Byatt's technique has a tight structure that might be called poetic but is actually more scientific in its careful, Victorian observation of order and pattern: her novellas have a character in common, a master mariner of mixed descent, who brings only a glancing presence to the book, and whose boat the Calypso carries the first novella's insect-observers beneath a night-sky full of illuminating stars, while in the second his supposed widow continues to find consolation in 'life and death' beneath the unlit, inky black of the sky and the sea off Margate. There are further parallels between the two tales: in one the Amazonian Indians are unable to conceive of a life other than on the banks of the river; in the other we learn of Cook's account of the New Zealand aboriginals, who simply could not perceive the ships when they arrived but were only too aware of the men climbing down from their hulls into the ship's boats. Everything is relative in science and religion.

But the most impressive part of the book is the account of the ant-watch in rural England, which the central characters write-up and get published as a kind of Desmond Morris project, well-researched and accessibly written. Eventually, after much wayward behaviour, including the discovery of his non-insectile wife flagrante delicto with her own brother, the first insect observer re-embarks for the Amazon with his stimulatingly ant-like mistress. The two novellas also use contemporary 19th century presences – of Darwin, Tennyson, and of John Clare – in a way which is strongly reminiscent, of course, of *Possession*. If I have a quibble it would be that the book is too determined, too loaded with contemporary lore and references, to succeed as a 19th century narrative: one can sometimes see the research sticking through (as you can in, for example, John Updike's *Roger's Version*). That said, life as an ant – as a mere cell in a ferociously community – is made to seem, dare I say it? more useful than life amongst the Brookner stick-insects in the mansion blocks of South Kensington.

JOHN HAYLOCK

Fabled Cities

Journey to Khiva by Philip Glazebrook
(Harvill. £15)

Like the boy in Walter Turner's poem,
'Romance', who was 'stolen away' by
Chimborazo and Kotopaxi, Philip
Glazebrook became fascinated by
Tashkent, Bokhara, Samarcand and
Khiva. Unlike the schoolboy, Glaze-
brook's dream was realized, but realiza-
tion brought disillusionment.

The passages that describe the past,
mainly nineteenth-century adventurers
and the rivalry between Britain and
Russia, are more colourful than those
which deal with the author's journey
through Uzbekistan.

In the chapter on Khiva, once an
oasis city, ruled over by a fierce and
cruel khan, a ruthless slave trader,
Glazebrook remarks that he was better
able to imagine what the place was like
when reading about it than when he was
actually there. Khiva has been 'killed',
as he puts it, by Russian restoration.
This once wild and perilous bastion has
become a museum for tourists, its
mosques and medressehs whitewashed.
Glazebrook had been to Russia before,
so the inconveniences and frustrations
of travelling in that land were not new to
him. However, he did not expect to be
attacked in the National Hotel in
Moscow by a marauder with a knife and
a cotton pad impregnated with ether.
He managed to fend off his assailant but

not without suffering severe cuts in the
face and hands. The staff of the hotel
were not helpful.

Scarred and shaken, he flew to
Tashkent, where he was met by Alex,
his interpreter, Anatoly, his driver, and
an Uzbek official, the head of the local
trade organization which arranged the
trips to the towns of Uzbekistan.

Viewed from the 30-story Intourist
Hotel, Tashkent, the Russian head-
quarters in Central Asia since it was
taken in 1865, has little left to remind
the visitor of its legendary past.
Glazebrook dwells much on the 'Great
Game', the 'game' of espionage and
challenge played by Russia and England
in the nineteenth century when Russia
coveted India. The Russian plan was
first to tame the tyrants who held sway
over Turkestan and then to advance on
India.

The British Government and the
East India Company were aware of
Russia's designs. In 1838 Colonel
Stoddart was sent to Bokhara with the
object of dissuading the Emir Nasrullah
from treating with the Russians. The
merciless murderous Emir imprisoned
him and also Captain Conolly, who went
to his rescue. Both had their throats cut.
Dr. Joseph Wolff, an eccentric Anglican
clergyman, set out in 1843 to Bokhara to
see if the two officers were alive. He
discovered they were not and managed
to get home unscathed.

'I never saw an uglier town', Glazebrook says of Samarcand, which seems
to consist of nothing but traffic and
concrete blocks. Later, though, when he
sees Tamerlane's sepulchre on his own
without an officious guide, he finds the

tomb 'compelling, humbling, with the magnetism of the true shrine'.

The most rewarding incident in the author's story was a picnic arranged by Anatoly, the driver, on a lake near Khiva. They crossed the wide 'sand coloured' Oxus, joined the driver's relations and friends and boarded a raft on which they had an uproarious party. Quantities of vodka were consumed. About this spirit, which the Russians introduced to Central Asia, Glazebrook, in spite of his quaffing huge draughts, says 'It is the drink of an unhappy race wanting no stops and no scenery on the way to oblivion'. Nevertheless, on the occasion of this picnic he found the company touchingly warm and hospitable.

Glazebrook admits that the reading he did about the Great Game, Central Asia and nineteenth-century Russia was 'browsing' rather than 'research'. His bibliography, however, is impressive. Of particular interest are the references to the notes made in the margins of Captain Conolly's prayer book, which was bought in a bazaar in Bokhara and mysteriously found its way into the hands of the Captain's sister in London. Also of interest is Captain James Abbott's account of his visit to Khiva, whither he was sent in 1839 to negotiate the release of the Russian slaves there. By doing so he hoped to eliminate the Russian need to capture the city.

Glazebrook does not mention, which he might well have done and it would have been of interest, how active Islam is today in this region, once ardently Muslim; also he uses the term Asiatic instead of the more acceptable Asian.

He writes well and his descriptions are effective, but while one is encouraged to read some of the volumes listed in the bibliography, the book does not give one an urge to go to Uzbekistan. The magic of the fabled cities has inevitably disappeared and they have become mundane and drably modern.

Captain Conolly, when he went on his abortive mission to rescue Stoddart, hoped to be able to persuade the despotic khans to form a federation against Russia. The author wonders if today the Captain's dream will materialize, for the inhabitants of the region feel they were exploited by the government of the Soviet Union.

JOHN MELLORS

Remaking Memories

The End of the Century at the End of the World by C. K. Stead (Harvill. £14.99)
The Promise of Light by Paul Watkins (Faber. £14.99)
Memories of Rain by Sunetra Gupta (Orion. £13.99)

The apocalyptic sound of C. K. Stead's title is misleading. It refers only to time and place: 1970 and 1990 in Auckland, New Zealand. The ending, indeed, is quite upbeat. On the last page, Laura, middle-aged mother of three, is about to begin writing a novel and remembering that someone had told her that the universe was 'self-correcting'.

The End of the Century at the End of the World can be enjoyed on several levels. On one it is a love-story, about a passionate affair between Laura and Dan, who came together at the end of the 'sixties and a year or two later quarrelled and separated. Laura had also been loved by a much older man, Maurice, although Maurice refrained from having sex with her even when he had the chance; he died in 1990. In the meantime Laura had married Roger, a lawyer, had three children, and left her husband after he had been unfaithful to her with Maurice's daughter. After the break-up with Laura Dan had gone into politics and by 1990 was a Cabinet Minister in the increasingly ineffectual Labour Government, soon to be defeated in a General Election.

On another level the book is a piece of literary detective work in the manner of *Possession* (A. S. Byatt is in fact one of two people to whom the book is dedicated). Did Katherine Mansfield live on for another thirty years, under an assumed name, after her supposed death in 1923? A third strand in the novel is about the way memory works. Stead believes that any *recherche du temps perdu* is an act in which we fictionalize the past; when we remember a past event we are making up a story about it. He illustrates this by giving us Dan's impression, in an auto-biographical fragment, of what had happened between him and Laura, and Laura's version of those events, which she had written in an unfinished novel. The two accounts, by the two protagonists, reveal how 'we all remake our memories, rewrite history to suit ourselves'.

When Dan first met Laura he was 27, a radical hippie, proprietor of 'the Anarchist Coffee Bar', ready to join in any protest, any demo, which was against the continuation of the Vietnam War. Laura was nine years his junior, and Dan was introduced to her by her father, a cheerful, bourgeois conservative, with whom Dan used to play tennis. Dan's memoir, '1970 – The Magic Bagwash', describes himself as having 'reddish hair and ginger opinions' and Laura as being 'the most desirable young woman I have ever encountered'. He ends the piece with an account of them both, still lovers, on a sandhill one evening: he hears her coming to him 'over dry sand that squeaks underfoot … Haven't we, Laura and I, at least for this moment, on warm sand and in sound of the sea, tilted the balance of forces in our universe a little towards the good?'

In Laura's fictional fragment there is an erotic scene in which Dave (Dan) sits naked on a bed, looking at Eve (Kiev, one of Dan's earlier girl-friends), who, also naked, is in a deep, post-coital sleep. Eve is an earth-mother, 'breasts large with pink, unassertive nipples', someone Dave sees as 'never there. She was away on a cloud. But she was a wonderful fuck'. In another scene, Larissa (Laura) is bitchy to Larry (Roger, whom Larry was to marry) and he walks out, leaving her crying. Laura can't recall whether that incident was fact or fiction: an instance where 'what you wrote became your memory', where fact was recomposed, becoming a story? Laura had ended her piece with Larissa quarrelling with Dave, telling him that she'd just been having 'an episode' and angrily suggesting that he should go to her flat-mate for sex in future: 'She's been wanting to suck your cock all term'.

Those two versions show Dan as more of a romantic, even idealist, but also perhaps more self-deceiving and less perceptive. Laura is both more sensitive and more realistic, but she is also more aggressive and wilfully destructive; she emphasizes the break-up while Dan stresses their earlier happiness. How much of that difference in attitude is that of two individuals and how much is intended to show inherent differences in the male and female temperament?

C. K. Stead has a gift for putting you in a particular place on a particular day, when you can almost read the barometer; 'It's late summer/early autumn – the sky clear, the sea windless. The dark red texture of Rangitoto, alight in shades of dark green and black, makes seeing seem like touching'. Stead makes reading seem like seeing and touching. The novel is by no means faultless. Laura is not quite 'round' enough for the prominence she is given in the story. Dan, the idealist trying hard to be taken for a pragmatist in politics, could with advantage have occupied the stage more often – together with Maurice, the mixed-up marxist who took his beloved to see the magic places of his boyhood and then slept happily beside her in a big brass bed without attempting to make love. There are minor irritants, too, like the dreams which Laura recounts and tries to explain or get others to explain. However, the good far outweighs the bad; the seeing and touching and the remaking of memories

turn *The End of the Century at the End of the World* into Stead's best novel since *All Visitors Ashore.*

The Promise of Light opens in 1921 on the coast of Rhode Island, New England. Young Ben Sheridan has just got a job in a bank and is pleased at the prospect of staying in the place he had always claimed as his own: 'The red-leafed autumns and the waves frozen green on the winter beaches and summer and spring were all wound up in my blood'. That blood is, in fact, to change his life for ever. His father is injured in a fire and when he receives Ben's blood in a transfusion it kills him. The incompatability proves that Ben can't have been his father's natural son. A family friend, Willoughby, the Catholic priest – 'Shaking the man's hand was like grabbing hold of a glove filled with pudding' – tells Ben that his father's wish had been to be cremated and for his ashes to be taken to Ireland and scattered on a beach near to where he had once lived. Ben decides to go and fulfil that dying wish and also find out who was his true father.

Paul Watkins is still in his twenties although this is his fourth novel. He is a confident writer, excelling in scenes of action. He writes about men who do hard manual work like trawling, farming, fighting, and is much less concerned with thinkers, artists or women. His style is terse, vigorous, fast-moving. Inevitably, he has been compared with Hemingway, but Watkins has a style of his own. He is more given to metaphors and other imagery and he does not go in for Hemingway's sometimes *faux naif* repetitions. A good example of his style is in the vivid immediacy with which he begins an episode, an immediacy at once masculine and colourful: 'I stood at the bow of the ferry, tasting salt that sprayed up in my face. Sunset turned the bay into a field of boiling copper'.

Ben arrives in Ireland only to find the ship on which Willoughby had secured his passage is gun-running for the IRA. As they are landing the crates on a lonely shore they are engaged in a skirmish with the Black and Tans. Ben is involved, like it or not, on the side of the IRA, and before long he knows that his best chance of survival is to stick with them and fight with them, however dangerous that might be. Watkins captures well the mixture in the Irish character: the idealism, melancholy, cynicism, sentimentality, cruelty, and, it would seem, a childish love of playing a real-life version of cops-and-robbers. There is also a defiant bloodymindedness: when the Black and Tans told Liz Gisby to paint God Bless the Black and Tans on the wall of her hotel or they'd burn it down, 'she painted it up, then burned the bloody place herself'.

Ben looks with wonder and distaste, and some admiration, at the men he's forced to trust. At Tarbox, the crabman, 'a dangerous and ugly man. It was as if he had been born in someone's nightmare, then kicked his way out of their head', and at Clayton, the ruthless, dedicated revolutionary: 'I couldn't imagine a childhood for Clayton. I couldn't imagine him younger or older or any way except the way he was now ... He didn't try like the others to live as if the war could be forgotten from time to time in the dark-panelled walls

of Gisby's pub or in front of a fire at night ... He saw no boundary to violence. The war never quit and his instinct for war never rested ...'

The fighting intensifies and Watkins rises to the occasion, his strong, swift prose reflecting and indeed magnifying the tension and excitement. Even when bullets and shells suggest he'll need luck to survive, Ben feels (as I think everyone does in the thick of action) that he will have that luck: 'It did not seem possible to me that all my thoughts could be snuffed out. I could imagine almost any degree of wounding and maiming and pain but not the simple vanishing of my mind'. How the fighting ends, and whether Ben ever finds his real father, must be left for the reader to enjoy discovering.

At the start of *Memories of Rain,* her first novel, Sunetra Gupta shows how fluently and stylishly she can write, as she describes how Moni meets the Englishman she was to marry. Moni's brother had brought Anthony to their house in Calcutta during the floods of '78, when 'the rain poured from the skies not to purify the earth but to spite it, to churn the parched fields into festering wounds, rinse the choked city sewers into the streets, sprinkle the pillows with the nausea of mold'; Anthony's 'alabaster calves' under his rolled-up jeans, and his 'large corpse-white, muck-rinded toes', had caused her 'to tremble in excitement and loathing'.

Unfortunately, it is not long before the writing becomes over-wrought and over-heated as a stream of consciousness clogs narrative and plot. The mandarin prose hither-and-thithers through courtship and marriage in India and infidelity in England and France and then back to shy adolescence and 'conservative Brahmanic habits' in Calcutta, before fast-forwarding again to 'the first taste of her long tryst with fear' in the gorges of the Ardeche, away, a long way away now, from that wedding night when, as Anthony slept, Moni had 'opened her wet thighs to darkness, to wash away her burning, to cleanse her'.

At her best, Sunetra Gupta writes a supple, sensuous prose, strikingly precise in its images and choice of detail, but too often she appears to be carried away by her own fluency and the style grows dense, almost opaque. You have to fish out the story from pools and eddies and cascades of words. Moni's family does not openly oppose her marriage but insists on a Bengali wedding, among themselves forecasting disaster. Anthony and Moni go to England. One year they go on holiday in France with Trevor, an old friend of Anthony, and Trevor's girl-friend, Anna. Anthony falls passionately in love with Anna while retaining an affectionate love for Moni. Moni gives birth to a daughter. Moni, Anna and Anthony live in an uneasy *ménage à trois*. Ten years after getting married Moni takes her child and flees back to India. We leave them after their arrival in Calcutta, in a taxi on Rashbehari Avenue, where 'the water has burst again, they say it is the curse of the Ganges, whose old course ran through that very spot'.

It has been a rough ride for the reader, highly enjoyable at times when Gupta comes up with bright images like 'little white flowers in her hair like strangled stars', but too often irritating when one is required to sympathize with Moni in her 'despair' that had 'acquired the velvet edges of a cosmic solitude'. Sunetra Gupta evidently loves writing and has great talent, but she will only do herself full justice when she can control her logophilia enough to keep free from logorrhoea.

JOHN RIZKALLA

Indian Slave

In an Antique Land by Amitav Ghosh (Granta Books. £14.99)

The puzzle is set: a tantalizing few letters, incomplete and torn: the twelfth century correspondence in Arabic between two prosperous Jewish merchants from Egypt. One trades in Aden, his partner in Mangalore. In one of the letters a Hindu Indian slave is singled out, unusually 'plentiful greetings' are extended to him. Soon he becomes a trusted business agent then a respected member of the household of Ben Yiju living in Southern India. Who was the slave? Even his name was not clear. Who were his masters? They wrote with such fluency, were judges in their communities. These people of different race and religion, working and living within the Muslim 'umma, exuded tolerance and harmony. We must remember that in 1148 the greatest

Crusader army ever was camped in the orchards of Damascus. Perhaps there was a lesson in all this for today.

These remnants of a much larger correspondence came to light eight hundred years later in Old Cairo, part of a collection of centuries-old manuscripts. In accordance with Jewish practice of the time and long after, members of the community deposited their writings in a Geniza (a storehouse rather than a library), to be disposed of with special rites. In this way the name of God, invoked in the writings, escaped desecration. By an extraordinary accident the Geniza of the obscure synagogue of Fustat was never cleared. Nor since the 9th century has that building been out of use as a place of worship. As with most things in History nothing is as obvious as it seems.

Amitav Ghosh is a Hindu and Anglo-Indian, a scholar in social anthropology. He came across the letters in 1981, and was in their grip for the next ten years (indeed despite writing to fine effect about them no doubt always will be). He decided to pursue his research in Egypt, and as a social anthropologist to combine it by living in the village of Lataifa in Lower Egypt. He kept a diary and many notes: *In an Antique Land* is the result.

Two distinct books emerge, though the author would like to connect them. In one 'story' the author is a sleuth, unearthing the Jewish merchant Ben Yiju, then the identity of his Indian slave. In the other he is writing an Egyptian 'Akenfield' minus the poetry, portraying life in a poorish village through a series of characters. It is an ambitious concept. Chapters from the two stories weave in and out of each other, often arbitrarily. A tenuous connection is made, almost inevitable in a fertile land which has attracted the retinues and retainers of History like weeds. Style and mood keep changing: a deceptive innocence for life among the villagers, mounting excitement as the sleuth pins down the past. Inevitably the seams show but since Amitav Ghosh makes both subject matters fascinating this does not matter too much. Whenever he can get on further in unravelling the past the author concentrates on the intense life around him. And makes a pleasing discovery: the stranger amidst them has become part of village life and gossip. For if the social anthropologist is observing he is no less in turn being weighed. What did these villagers make of this sophisticated man? One of the skills and fascinations of the book is how they come to perceive him. The irony of course is that having done so they are convinced their guest is inferior and rush to raise him up to their own beliefs. The villagers were exclusively Muslim and knew something about Jews and Christians from the Koran. But Hindus? Although speaking Arabic the author finds it near impossible (interesting insight into how Arabic and Islam are shown to be inextricable) to convey the significance of cremation. Burning corpses as if they were straw simply horrifies his Muslim hosts. Nor can the scholar rise above a stammer when an irate Imam accuses him of the scandalous worship of cows. Yet Islam in the village is not pure. The cult of saints, visiting the grave of the local marabout, invoking his favours, these are practices the Muslims share with Christians, if not the Jewish congregation in Fustat.

Beyond the description of village life and customs what makes the narrative are the finely observed characters. They come alive when they speak, friendly and angry towards each other, sharing family problems we recognize, unashamedly with the author and us. Years later when the narrator returns unannounced to Lataifa, in the middle of the night and a power cut, Sheikh Musa does not hesitate to get out of bed and welcome him into his home. It's the same instinctive hospitality which can pick up the life story of each one as if there had been no absence. There is a long cast: the landlord Abu Ali who resembled an engorged python, the important Khamees the Rat, Ustaz Sabry the schoolmaster, Taha the witch, Zaghloul the Weaver, the querulous Imam, friends who opened their lives to the narrator. The young men who left the village to seek their fortune in Iraq where (a universal story) the locals resented and often mounted attacks on them. They came back, though, rich enough to modernize the family home and achieve their highest ambition, marriage to a city girl. The Klondyke has of course not lasted, typified poignantly by Nabeel, the last character mentioned in the book. Like countless other Egyptian labourers he ended up as flotsam in the Gulf War.

The narrator resists the villagers' entreaties to become a Muslim, indeed is most careful not to give away any of his own beliefs (managing to irritate at times not just his hosts but the reader), prefers to record than to act. He is the innocent abroad, limiting his vision and concerns to that of the village. But in a last excursion, seeking to visit a marabout's grave which turns out to be one venerated by Muslim and Jews alike, he is subjected to a nasty arrest. The Egyptian idyll is savaged. In an earlier and fine chapter the narrator recalls his terror as a child when Muslims besieged him and his family in Dakkah. He concludes that the villagers in Egypt were 'far gentler, far less violent, very much more humane and innocent than mine'. An odd reading when one remembers that with the rise of fundamentalism violent and bloody sectarian incidents were occurring at the time of his narrative and since in at least Upper Egypt.

What of the 'raison d'être' of the book? The Indian slave so honoured by his Jewish masters? His is an intriguing story and like all good mysteries goes from surprise to surprise. At the end, though, again like all true quests, the author is left with new and tantalizing questions. In the process an impeccable scholar has delighted as he instructed.

ALMA HROMIC

Encoded Messages

A World of My Own: A Dream Diary by Graham Greene (Reinhardt Books. £12.99)

In his novel *The Power and the Glory,* Graham Greene writes of how 'The glittering worlds lay there in space like a promise; the world was not the universe. Somewhere Christ may not have died.' If such a place exists, Greene's long-time lady companion, Yvette Cloetta, says in her Introduction, then Greene has certainly found it. That is beyond question; so, probably, has every reader of this book. In every human being there is a private universe where one god or another from a private pantheon is alive and well, following some very public crucifixion. The question is, would that universe interest any other human being – and should it be expected to do so.?

This, of course, is a posthumous book, and despite the pious platitudes about the joy brought to the dying literary giant's final days by choosing and arranging the material to be included in it, perhaps its real motives ought to be examined a little more closely. Yes, there are things in it which are deeply interesting, given the identity of the dreamer. Any insight into the workings of a mind like Greene's is fascinating, especially where it concerns the genesis of his literary *oeuvre*. The trouble is that there is not enough of this, and far too much of the kind of dream which ends with '. . . and of what happened next I have no memory.' The literary device of '. . . and then I woke up. . .' is as old and trite as any hoary literary cliché you care to name, and Greene of all people should have known this. He also exhibits a somewhat unnerving obsession with piscine life, dreaming bizarre encounters with prawns and langoustines – a psychologist would have a field day. We are treated to staccato encounters

with dead writers and dead or living politicians, princes and statesmen who crossed Greene's path during the course of his tempestous and fascinating life – and, in the case of the writers, influenced him and his work. There are also some religious encounters, including a visit to the Pope to make a deeply important confession – which remained unsaid because the Pontiff turned out to be asleep at the time of Greene's arrival. Given Greene's own well-publicised views on the Catholic religion, all kinds of interesting inferences can be drawn from this.

This is nothing like vintage Graham Greene. The author himself offers very little insight into his private universe – his dreams are simply trotted out, rather baldly, and the reader is left to put the pieces together. As an exercise in writing, this certainly does not engage its author's full powers or the incisive mind revealed in so many other of Greene's works: it is very much a private 'diary', written for Greene's own interest and benefit. The reader will probably learn nothing of major importance about Graham Greene the writer or the man, aside from personal insights which require a certain amount of prior knowledge to be in any way useful. At the same time, dreams have been deeply interesting to the human race ever since language evolved into an instrument sensitive enough to record their nuances. Dreams of great men, especially those we have made great through the public acclamation of their gifts, are therefore doubly absorbing.

It would be very easy to dismiss this book as a simple attempt to cash in on